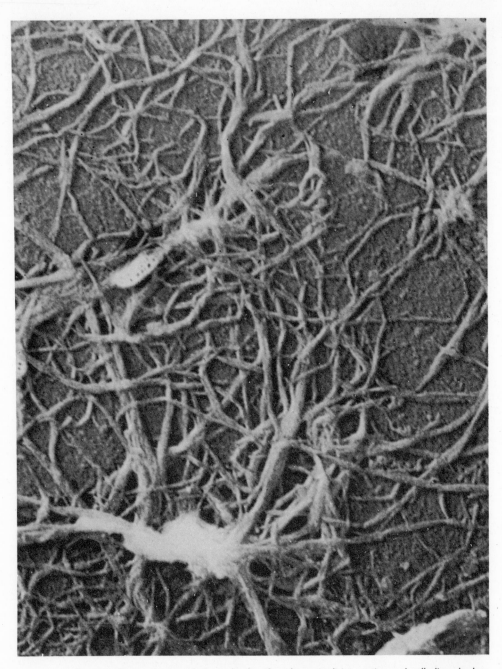

Electron micrograph of purified wood pulp, after ultrasonic disintegration and palladium shadowing. 100,000X. (Courtesy Frederick F. Morehead, Research and Development Division, American Viscose Corporation)

# FUNDAMENTALS

# OF

# HIGH POLYMERS

O. A. BATTISTA

*Research and Development Division*
*American Viscose Corporation*
*Marcus Hook, Pennsylvania*

**REINHOLD PUBLISHING CORPORATION**

NEW YORK

CHAPMAN & HALL, LTD., LONDON

Copyright 1958 by
REINHOLD PUBLISHING CORPORATION

---

Library of Congress Catalog Number 58-10427

REINHOLD PUBLISHING CORPORATION

*Publishers of Chemical Engineering Catalog, Chemical Materials Catalog, "Automatic Control," "Materials in Design Engineering," "Progressive Architecture;" Advertising Management of the American Chemical Society*

Printed in U.S.A. by
THE GUINN CO., INC.
New York 1, N. Y.

## ACKNOWLEDGMENT

The author wishes to express his appreciation of the cooperation of the management of American Viscose Corporation in helping to make this textbook possible. His thanks are extended, in particular, to Dr. Herschel H. Cudd, Vice President, Research and Development Division, for his personal interest and encouragement, and to the many members of the research staff with whom the author has had occasion to explore the science of high polymers during the past eighteen years.

To those scientists who have so painstakingly un-
veiled the exciting and far-reaching complications
of the structure and mechanism of high polymers.

# Preface

Cotton and wool, nylon and silk, pulp and paper, "Dacron" and "Mylar," "Acrilan" and "Orlon," rubbers, lacquers, and plastics, rayons and cellophanes—these and an almost endless list of other products are the materials that give growing importance to the science of high polymers. Many billion dollars worth of these products are made each year. Numerous industries and millions of people are sustained by these remarkable materials, all of which are comprised of long-chain molecules. These not only constitute the cornerstone of high polymer chemistry and physics, but also are the essence of living processes as seen in proteins and nucleic acids which are the bases of life itself.

The union of simple molecules into long chains, very much as one might hook many paper clips together to construct a snake-like ribbon, appears to be the underlying mechanism whereby so many materials around us acquire their ultimate physical form. It is the bunching together or aggregation of ever-increasing numbers of these long chains of simple molecules that is the common denominator underlying the molecular architecture of all high polymer products.

During the past two or three decades the technology and commercialization of high polymers has advanced with remarkable speed. Attention to practical results that have emerged from industrial laboratories has been so concentrated that undergraduate study of high polymer science has not kept pace with the demands of industry. Except for a few high polymer institutes scattered throughout the world, most of which are designed to train scientists and engineers at the graduate level, there are few, if any, academic courses offered on high polymer chemistry and physics.

This book has been designed and written with the hope that it may serve as an introductory textbook for courses on high polymers at the undergraduate level. A broad spectrum of high polymer technology is covered to provide a view of the commercially important products in this field. A generous supply of schematic illustrations has been included in an effort to make certain high polymer concepts more understandable for the beginner.

As is the case with any science which grows rapidly, there exists in the literature on high polymers today a great deal of ambiguity and confusion regarding the terms and definitions which are an integral part of high polymer language. Unless students of this new science, as well as those who may be approaching it for the first time as professional people, are able to gain a clear understanding of the characteristic nomenclature of this subject, what follows in the text may be much more difficult to grasp. It is for these reasons that an attempt has been made to present in the beginning of the book the best definitions available for the key terms of high polymer science.

Chapters on the basic chemistry of all of the major natural and man-made high polymer products follow the definitions of the key terms. The formation of useful macromolecular products and details of their interesting architecture are described. Following this, there are sections on the measurement of both the solution and solid state properties of high polymers, and also their physical properties as related to specific end uses. Finally, an extensive bibliography is included.

This book might also serve as a handy reference for chemists, engineers, physicists, and biologists engaged in academic research or industrial high polymer technology. It is also the author's hope that management executives, supervisory personnel, and chemists and engineers entering the high polymer industries for the first time may find the book useful as a means of familiarizing themselves with the fundamentals of the science upon which their products are based, and as a basis for the easier understanding of the many excellent works on high polymers that are highly specialized.

O. A. Battista

Marcus Hook, Pennsylvania
April 1958

# CONTENTS

# Part I

# BASIC PRINCIPLES
# OF
# HIGH POLYMERS

# 1. Basic Terms and Definitions

A set of key terms and clear definitions is an important requisite for the understanding of any science; and this is especially true in the case of a science as new as high polymers. Since the basic terms and definitions that are the cornerstones of the "language" of high polymers are a logical starting point for the beginner, we are placing them at the beginning of the book. A little time spent now in acquiring a familiarity with these key definitions will make the science of high polymers much easier to assimilate as well as more fascinating.

The nomenclature of high polymers has been assembled in alphabetical order so that it will be convenient to refer back to specific definitions. As an understanding of the language characteristics of high polymer science is acquired, the knowledge behind myriad useful high polymer products that are playing an increasingly important role in your daily life will unfold.

## Crystallite (see Fibril, Micelle)

When two or more long-chain molecules come close enough together laterally to lock in any way, the nucleus of a *crystallite* is born and a crystallite begins to grow. A crystallite consists of a cluster of associated long-chain molecules that make up a more or less regular structural unit, or building block, out of which a particular high polymer is constructed. In other words, it is the basic micro-unit of the geometric architecture of high polymers. The size varies over a wide range—from the order of tens to hundreds of Angstrom units (see Figure 1). Crystallites can increase or decrease in size without a significant change in their chemical make-up. The long-chain molecules in crystallites are so tightly packed that even beams of x-rays directed at them are readily diffracted. It is usually

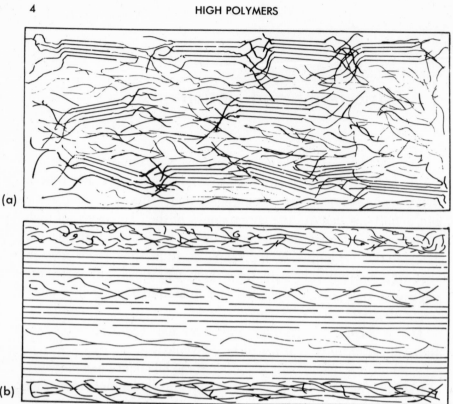

(a)

(b)

Figure 1. Typical fine structures for fibrous high polymers showing small and large crystallite areas, respectively.
   (a) Small crystalline areas embedded in a network.
   (b) Large parallel crystalline areas separated by disordered long chains.

by means of this structural characteristic that the size of crystallites is determined experimentally.

## Degree of Polymerization (D.P.)

The *degree of polymerization* (D.P.) is the average number of repeating units in a linear macromolecule, if such a macromolecule consists of regularly repeating units; or, the average number of mers (monomeric units) per macromolecule if such a long chain molecule is built up of identical monomers. The D.P. is determined by dividing the (average) molecular weight of the monomer into the molecular weight of the macromolecule.

### Elastomer (or Rubber)

*Elastomer* is a term that refers to non-crystalline high polymers or rubbers that have a three-dimensional space-network structure (e.g., vulcanization) which imparts stability or resistance to plastic deformation. Normally, elastomers exhibit long-range elasticity (rubber band effect) at ordinary room temperatures.

### Fiber

A *fiber* is a thread or thread-like structure composed of fine strings or filaments of linear macromolecules that are intertwined or associated in such a manner as to give rise to an assemblage of molecules having a high ratio of length to width. The dual structure of ordered and disordered regions coupled with the orientation of these regions is known as "fiber structure."

### Fibril (see Crystallite, Micelle)

A *fibril* consists essentially of an aggregate of micelles or crystallites that is large enough to appear like a very fine fiber under a high-power microscope. In the extreme case, of course, a fibril and a large micelle or crystallite may be considered synonymous. Normally, however, a fibril is an aggregate of many crystallites connected by long chain molecules that may run continuously between several of the component crystallites (see Figure 1).

In modern times, two main schools of thought have grown up regarding the basic nature of fibrils. On the one hand, there are those who believe that fibrils are "preformed" to a characteristic size or dimension. The other group argues that fibrils are a natural consequence of the aggregation of long-chain molecules. If the formation of micelles—i.e., more or less discrete aggregates of molecules —is a reflection of an optimum thermodynamic state, then it may be said that both schools of thought are belaboring the same basic point. A third point of view is worth mentioning. It is true that the size of "micelles" or "fibrils" found after destructive chemical attack on a polymer is influenced by the severity of the treatment. If these ultimate units of fiber or film structures reduce to finer and

finer strands with increasingly severe chemical treatment, then it is
conceivable, at least, that the true ultimate fibril is a single long-
chain molecule.

### Film

A *film* is a relatively thin skin, membrane, or pellicle less than
10 mils thick which usually is transparent or translucent.

### Glass

In the broadest sense, a solid mass comprised of long-chain
molecules that is transparent or translucent is termed a *glass*. In
essence, glasses are considered to be supercooled liquids in which
the long chain or macromolecules exhibit local regularities in
structure only over relatively short ranges.

### High Polymer

By convention, the term *high polymer* includes all materials
whose chemical and physical structures depend on the arrangement
in sequence of many monomers (identical or similar groups of
atoms) connected by primary chemical bonds to form long chains
or macromolecules. Aggregations of these long chains yield useful
products which have more or less distinctive characteristics such
as tensile strength, extensibility, elastic recovery, and many others.

The macromolecules that make up a high polymer consist of
multiples of lower molecular weight units. The repeating units
(*monomers* or *mers*) in the long chain macromolecule do not all have
to be of the same size, nor do they have to possess exactly the same
composition or chemical structure. Differences in composition and
chemical structure in the units in the long chains of a high polymer
arise from occasional branches, the presence of end groups, and
other irregularities.

By way of clarifying different terms used by English speaking
scientists and those in the continental European countries, it should
be pointed out that the terms "high polymer" and "macromolecular
substance" have the same meaning. Staudinger coined the word
"macromolecule" to identify long chain molecules prior to 1930,

and it has enjoyed wide usage on the Continent ever since. The term "high polymer" is more commonly used in Great Britain and the United States.

High polymer substances in general may be subdivided into several major types and classes:

**Block Copolymer.** In a block copolymer the repeating units consist of segments or blocks of similar monomers tied together along the macromolecular chain. This differs somewhat from copolymers (see below) where the repeating unit consists of two or more different single monomers.

**Branched High Polymer.** This polymer is one in which the long chain molecule is not uniformly straight like a pencil, but has branches extending from its trunk as shown in Figure 2. The long-

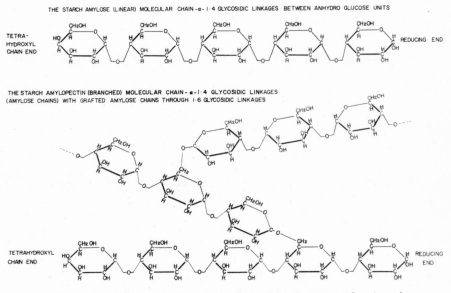

Figure 2.　Schematic drawings of straight-chain (amylose) and branched-chain (amylose pectin) starch molecules.

chain molecule, despite these branches, remains unattached to other similar molecules surrounding it.

**Copolymer.** This is the term applied to a long-chain molecule comprised of at least two *different* monomers joined together in irregular sequence. A typical example of a copolymer is the textile fiber "Vinyon." This fiber consists of a series of vinyl acetate and vinyl chloride molecules repetitively joined together in a hand-in-glove arrangement. In contrast to this, a physical mixture of poly-ethylene and polypropylene macromolecules, for example, is *not* a copolymer, but simply a *mixture* of homopolymers.

Segments of two separate "Vinyon" molecules are compared in Figure 3. Attention is called to the acetate group projecting from

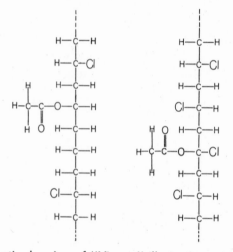

Figure 3. Schematic drawing of "Vinyon" illustrating a typical copolymer.

the side of the molecule in the right hand formula; steric hindrance would prevent the chain segment from packing closely with the chain segment represented by the left hand formula.

**Cross-linked High Polymers.** These polymers are those in which the long-chain molecules—either straight or branched—have ladder-rungs or cross bridges binding them together as shown in Figure 4 (see also Figure 9, p. 46). In this type of high polymer, all or most of the component long chain molecules are rigidly locked to each other laterally by primary linkages (e.g., wool, Figure 4). This is different from "space-network" polymers, where the cross-bonding between chains proceeds along three-dimensional rather than by two-dimensional or lateral planes. In practice, however, the term

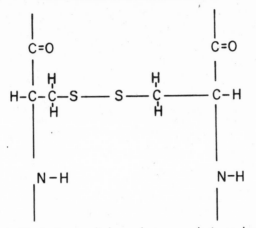

Figure 4. Typical cross-linkage between chain molecules—
the cystine bridge in wool.

"cross-linked" polymer is sometimes applied to both (see **Space-network High Polymer** below).

**Derived High Polymer.** When a primary high polymer or a natural high polymer is altered chemically (so as to produce a derivative) it is called a derived high polymer.

**Graft Copolymer.** When a given kind of monomer is polymerized and, subsequently, another kind of monomer is polymerized onto the primary high polymer chain, a graft copolymer results.

**High Polymeric (or Macromolecular) Compound.** By convention, this term is more specific than the broad category of "high polymer." It is used to describe a substance consisting of a composite of long-chain molecules that are *alike* in composition, chemical structure, and size.

**Primary High Polymer.** This type of polymer is produced by the polymerization of chemically identical monomers into long chains, without subsequently altering the chemical nature of the resulting macromolecules.

**Space-network High Polymer.** When there are two or more reactive functional groups in the *monomer* or *mer* building block, the growth of the polymer in three dimensions is possible during the course of the polymerization. Such a process gives rise to a space-network high polymer. A good illustration is the reaction between glycerol and phthalic anhydride, which yields a three-dimensional network polymer (see p. 38). Other examples are thermosetting plastics such as the phenol-formaldehyde and the urea-formaldehyde types, respectively.

**Stereoregular High Polymers:** *Atactic Polymer.* When the R-groups or substituent groups are positioned on all sides of the main backbone of a long-chain molecule in a completely random manner, an "atactic" polymer results, as shown in Figure 5. Such

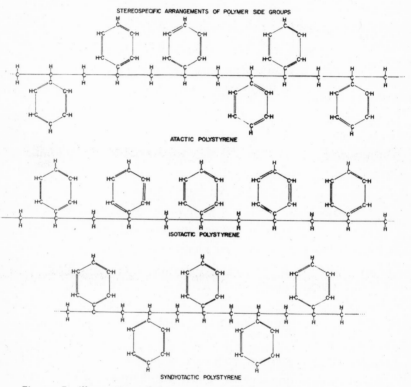

STEREOSPECIFIC ARRANGEMENTS OF POLYMER SIDE GROUPS

ATACTIC POLYSTYRENE

ISOTACTIC POLYSTYRENE

SYNDYOTACTIC POLYSTYRENE

Figure 5. Illustration of three stereospecific configurations of the polystyrene molecule: atactic, isotactic, and syndiotactic.

molecules cannot pack tightly together because of steric hindrance, and result in soft, non-crystalline and rather gummy products.

*Isotactic Polymer.* An isotactic polymer is one in which the R-groups or substituent groups *all* lie either above or below the main backbone of the long-chain molecule. Such an arrangement (sometimes referred to as stereoregular) makes possible a very highly ordered or compact high polymer, one that crystallizes readily (see Figure 5).

*Syndiotactic (or Syndyotactic) Polymer.* When the R-groups or substituent groups occupy positions that alternate regularly and in sequence above and below the main backbone of a long-chain molecule, a syndiotactic polymer results (see Figure 5). Such an arrangement permits relatively easy packing of the long-chain molecules and gives rise to substances whose properties lie between those of an isotactic and an atactic polymer, respectively.

## Macromolecule. See discussion under High Polymer
## Micelle (see also Fibril, Crystallite)

A *micelle* is an aggregation of crystallites of colloidal dimensions that exist either in the solid state or in solution. It represents a reasonably reproducible dimension as the result of uniform chemical or mechanical treatments. It is sometimes used synonymously with the term "crystallite." It is very probable that a particular polymer micelle is an aggregation of long chains, reflecting the most stable state (thermodynamically) as the individual molecules pack from a solution or melt to form a solid product under a given environment.

## Molecule (see also Monomeric Unit)

In the classic sense, a *molecule* is the smallest part of a substance that can exist separately and still retain a unique identity. This, in essence, defines a molecule as two or more atoms that are held together by primary or atom-to-atom bonds to produce a specific compound. On the basis of this definition, therefore, a diamond or piece of quartz might exist as a single molecule, just as could the simple gas oxygen ($O_2$).

## Monomeric Unit or Mer

All high polymers are formed by the joining together of many molecular units (as in polyethylene) or of *groups* of molecular units as illustrated in the case of cellulose (see Figure 6). The *monomeric unit* or *mer* of a linear high polymer is the *unit* of the molecule which contains the same kinds and numbers of atoms as the real or hypothetical repeating unit.

The monomeric unit (or mer) of a linear high polymer is not, therefore, necessarily a "molecule." The repeating unit of many linear polymers is a distinct segment of the molecular chain. The complete macromolecule (neglecting minor irregularities at the ends, branch junctions, etc.) might conceivably consist of a large number of these units, oriented in the longitudinal axis of the chain.

## Polymer

A *polymer* in its broadest sense is a product formed by the combination of the same elements in the same proportions, but differing from the original "building blocks" in molecular weight. For example, cyanuric acid, $C_3N_3O_3H_3$, is a polymer of cyanic acid, CNOH, three molecules of CNOH combining to form $C_3N_3O_3H_3$. Similarly, paraformaldehyde $(CH_2O)_n$ is a polymer of formaldehyde $CH_2O$, in which $n$ molecules of $(CH_2O)$ combine to give a new product or polymer $(CH_2O)_n$. (See **High Polymer.**)

## Polymerization

The term "polymerization" refers to the *process* of formation of large molecules from smaller molecules, with or without the simultaneous formation of other products, such as water. (See **Polymer.**)

Some kinds of molecules, like ethylene $(CH_2{=}CH_2)$, can react with themselves to form uniform long chain molecules, for example, $-CH_2-CH_2-CH_2-CH_2-CH_2-$ (polyethylene). In other cases two kinds of monomers react, forming *copolymers*.

*Polyaddition.* Polyaddition occurs when small molecules join each other, under the stimulus of a catalyst or a free radical mechanism to form linear polymers, usually *without* the coincident formation of by-product molecules. The formation of polyethylene from ethylene is a classic example.

*Polycondensation.* Polycondensation is a special type of polymerization commonly called C-polymerization. It refers to the union of monomers involving a chemical change, namely, release, or "splitting off" of simple molecules (such as $H_2O$ or $NH_3$) coincident with the formation of macromolecules. The polycondensation of glucose by bacteria to produce long chain cellulose molecules with loss of a molecule of water is a typical example of this kind of polymerization. The formation of nylon by the polycondensation of hexamethyldiamine and adipic acid is a classic example of a synthetic high polymer produced by means of this type of polymerization (see Table 3, p. 36).

## Resin

A *resin* is a high polymeric compound which will not crystallize, is insoluble in water but soluble in some organic solvents, softens with heat, and may be a very viscous liquid or a solid at room temperature. Solid resins and thermoplastics are very similar, with physical state and properties at room temperature serving as the differentiating basis.

## Spherulite

The term *spherulite* is being used in high polymer science in a sense paralleling its original definition, which refers to spherical crystalline bodies made up of radiating crystalline patterns like those found in mixtures of quartz and feldspar. A spherulite results from the aggregation of partly oriented crystallites that radiate outward from a common point to produce a pattern like butterfly wings. One characteristic of a spherulite structure is that the crystallographic axis of each of the component crystallites points outward somewhat like the spokes in a wheel.

# 2. Chemistry of High Polymers

## Cellulose

Cellulose, the snow-white carbohydrate material that we see so frequently in the form of cotton, paper, rayon, and numerous plastics, is the most abundant organic material in the world. It is the primary substance that supports the entire vegetable kingdom. For example, without cellulose a tree would have no support; it could not withstand the tremendous weight of its branches and leaves. The same is true of a rose bush, or a blade of grass. It is the cellulose in all plant life which provides the *structural* properties that the plant possesses—its rigidity and its ability to take a form or shape and hold it.

Americans alone use more than ten times as much cellulose as they do aluminum and copper combined. This is completely apart from the billions of tons of raw cellulose that form the bulk in the diet of beef cattle, dairy cows, horses, and other forms of animal life. As a matter of fact, cellulose is probably the most vital raw material for the sustenance and welfare of mankind. In view of its importance, we are examining the chemistry of cellulose in greater detail than its carbohydrate relatives.

Cellulose is made from water and carbon dioxide gas, which contain the three elements necessary for carbohydrate formation—carbon, oxygen, and hydrogen. With the aid of chlorophyll and sunlight, water and carbon dioxide gas react to form a sweet substance called glucose, more commonly known as "grape sugar"; when recovered from the sap of the maple tree, it is the familiar "maple sugar."

The next step in the transformation of these commonplace substances to cellulose is a binding together of the individual molecules of glucose, end on end, to form long strings; in this process (called polycondensation), one molecule of water is lost from each glucose macromolecule. This results in the formation of a cellulose molecule.

Imagine a paper clip to be one molecule of glucose minus a molecule of water (a monomer). A single molecule of cellulose in rayon, for example, could be represented by stringing approximately 500 of the paper clips together into a long chain. Cellulose in cotton, on the other hand, exists as a much longer chain; as many as 3,000 to 5,000 paper clips would be needed to describe a single macromolecule in cotton as it exists in the natural state.

Next, these long chains unite to produce crystallites which may be likened to beads on a string. The strings of crystallites in turn combine to form fibrils or tiny filaments, very much in the fashion of grouping together a bunch of matchsticks. When this "aggregation" of long chains is accomplished by nature or by man, a filament or fiber makes its physical appearance. Each little filament of rayon, for example, even though it is barely visible to the eye, has more than 100,000 individual long cellulose chains bunched together like pencils or matchsticks!

All cellulose, therefore, is essentially 100 per cent glucose. One explanation of why it doesn't taste sweet or doesn't dissolve in water is that the long-chain cellulose molecules are so tightly grouped together in bundles. If these bunches are dissolved by chemical treatment and the long chains subdivided into the glucose molecules from which they are made, the cellulose loses its fibrous nature, swells, and dissolves in water.

In this truly remarkable natural high polymer we have a prototype—an almost ideal example—upon which may be based numerous parallels for explaining most of the other natural and man-made high polymer systems. A schematic as well as an atomic model of the chemical structure of the cellulose molecule is shown in Figure 6. A side-by-side comparison of its chemical composition with some man-made long-chain molecules—"Dacron," nylon, and polyethylene—is presented in Figure 7.

The monomer, or repeating unit in the cellulose molecule, the

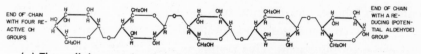

(a) The cellulose molecular chain (5 monomer units): $\beta$-1, 4-glycosidic linkages between anhydroglucose units.

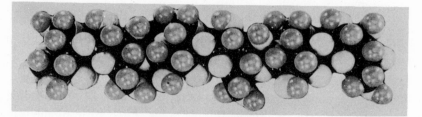

(b) Atomic model—side view (6 monomer units).

(c) Atomic model—top view (6 monomer units).

Figure 6. Schematic and atomic models of a cellulose chain.

glucose-minus-$H_2O$-unit, has the formula $C_6H_7O_2(OH)_3$, or more commonly $C_6H_{10}O_5$, which corresponds to a molecular weight of 162. It is identical in *chemical* composition with the monomer unit in the straight-chain starch molecule (amylose):

MONOMERIC UNIT

CELLULOSE OR STARCH (AMYLOSE)

Formula          Molecular Wt.

$[C_6H_7O_2(OH)_3]_n$          $[162]_n$
or $(C_6H_{10}O_5)_n$

$$(CO_2)_x + (H_2O)_x$$

$$\downarrow \text{sunlight}$$

$$[(-C_6H_{10}O_5-)]_n$$

## Starch

Chemically, starch is a "blood relative" of cellulose. The intimate chemical similarity between starch and cellulose has, never-

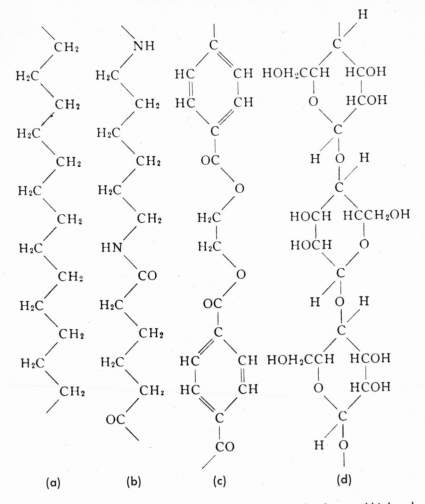

Figure 7. Side-by-side comparison of schematic models of several high polymer molecules: (a) polyethylene, (b) nylon, (c) "Dacron," and (d) cellulose.

theless, little effect on the respective physical properties of these two substances. Here we have an excellent example of how important the posture or molecular geometry of chemically similar or identical long-chain molecules can be in determining the usefulness of high polymeric products.

Natural starches usually consist of at least two distinct types of carbohydrate polymers—the straight-chain or linear type known as *amylose,* and the branched-chain variety known as *amylopectin.* Although the average proportion of amylose in natural starches is generally of the order of 20 to 30 per cent, in recent years hybrid corns have been developed in which the proportion of amylose has been increased to 70 to 80 per cent. Recent research on the fractionation of starches has revealed that there are at least three and maybe four distinct carbohydrate species in natural starches. Amylose and amylopectin, however, are the only two that have been studied extensively up to this time.

Whereas cellulose largely forms the structural backbone of plant materials, starch is the energy-reserve material which concentrates in roots and seeds. It is, of course, the foundation material for numerous cereals, a raw material for the fermentation industries, and a valuable sizing compound for the paper and textile industries.

The straight-chain component in starch, amylose, consists only of $\alpha$-1-4, glycosidic bonds. Amylopectin, the branched-chain component in starch, consists of the same $\alpha$-1-4 linkage of anhydroglucose units *along with* periodic branching or grafting onto the base amylose chain through 1:6 linkages of other amylose chains. A comparison of the cellulose, starch amylose, and starch amylopectin structures is made in Figures 2 and 6. As may be seen, the only difference between the cellulose chain and the amylose chain is in the nature of the linkages between the anhydroglucose units; $\beta$-1-4 for cellulose, and $\alpha$-1-4 for amylose.

## Alginic Acid

Alginic acid, present in the cell walls of certain brown seaweeds, is in itself only sparingly soluble in water. As the sodium salt, however, it is very soluble in water and falls into the use category of such thickening agents and gum substitutes as CMC and methyl cellulose. The calcium salt, on the other hand, is soluble in dilute alkalies, and textile fibers can be spun from it. Structurally, alginic acid resembles cellulose closely, except that a —COOH group is present in place of the primary hydroxyl group —$CH_2OH$.

FORMULA FOR ALGINIC ACID

| Monomer Unit | Structural Formula | Molecular Weight of Mer |
|---|---|---|
| $-(C_6H_8O_6)-$ | | 176 |

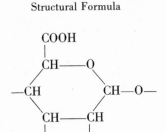

## Chitin

Although chitin is not a true carbohydrate, it is included here because, as a naturally occurring aminopolysaccharide, it is potentially attractive from a chemical standpoint. Chitin resembles cellulose structurally and occurs in nature primarily as the material out of which the horny part or protective armor of insects, lobsters, and crabs is made.

FORMULA FOR CHITIN

(Not a true carbohydrate)

| Monomer Unit | Structural Formula | Molecular Weight of Mer |
|---|---|---|
| $-(C_8H_{13}O_5NH)-$ | | 204 |

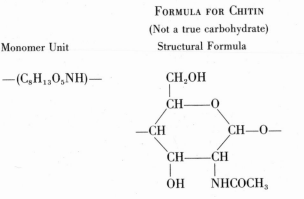

## COMMERCIAL DERIVATIVES OF CELLULOSE

Although cellulose *per se* is a very important commodity, tremendous tonnages of its various derivatives are used annually. A brief description of each of the most important commercial cellulose esters and ethers follows. Table 1 illustrates the reactions whereby these derivatives are formed, and Table 2 is a compilation

TABLE 1.  FORMATION OF CELLULOSE DERIVATIVES—ESTERS AND ETHERS

| High Polymer | Monomeric Unit Formula | Molecular Wt. | General Reaction to Form Polymer or Polymer Derivative |
|---|---|---|---|
| CELLULOSE (TRI-) NITRATE (ESTER) | $-[C_6H_7O_2-(O-NO_2)_3]_n-$ | 297 | $C_6H_7O_2(OH)_3 + \begin{bmatrix} H_2SO_4 \\ HNO_3 \end{bmatrix} \rightarrow$ $[-C_6H_7O_2-(ONO_2)_3]$ |
| CELLULOSE (TRI-) ACETATE (ESTER) | $-[C_6H_7O_2-(OCOCH_3)_3]_n-$ | 288 | $C_6H_7O_2(OH)_3 + 3(CH_3CO)_2O$ $[-C_6H_7O_2-(OCOCH_3)_3-]$ $+ 3CH_3COOH$ |
| CELLULOSE (TRI-) XANTHATE (ESTER) | $-[C_6H_7O_2-(OCS_2H)_3]_n-$ | 396 | (1) $C_6H_{10}O_5 + NaOH \rightarrow$ $C_6H_9O_4 \cdot ONa + H_2O$<br>(2) $C_6H_9O_4 \cdot ONa + CS_2 \rightarrow$ $CS\begin{matrix} SNa \\ O \cdot C_6H_9O_4 \end{matrix}$<br>(3) $CS\begin{matrix} SNa \\ O \cdot C_6H_9O_4 \end{matrix} + HOH \rightarrow CS\begin{matrix} SH \\ O \cdot C_6H_9O_4 \end{matrix} + NaOH$<br>*Note:* Reaction shows formation of the mono-substituted derivative. |

| Name | Structure | No. | Reaction |
|---|---|---|---|
| CELLULOSE (TRI-) ETHYLATE (ETHER) (ETHYL CELLULOSE) | $-[C_6H_7O_2-(OC_2H_5)_3]_n-$ | 246 | $C_6H_7O_2(OH)_3 + 3C_2H_5Cl + 3NaOH$ (Pressure) $\rightarrow [-C_6H_7O_2-(OC_2H_5)_3] + 3NaCl + 3H_2O$ |
| CELLULOSE (TRI-) METHYLATE (ETHER) (METHYL CELLULOSE) | $-[C_6H_7O_2-(OCH_3)_3]_n-$ | 204 | $C_6H_7O_2(OH)_3 + 3CH_3Cl + NaOH$ (Pressure) $\rightarrow [-C_6H_7O_2-(OCH_3)_3] + NaCl + H_2O$ |
| CELLULOSE (TRI-) CARBOXYMETHYLATE (ETHER) (CARBOXYMETHYL CELLULOSE) | $-[C_6H_7O_2-(OCH_2COOH)_3]_n-$ | 336 | $C_6H_7O_2(OH)_3 + 3CH_2(Cl)COOH + NaOH \rightarrow [-C_6H_7O_2-(OCH_2COOH)_3] + NaCl + H_2O$ |
| CELLULOSE (TRI-) HYDROXYETHYLATE (ETHER) (HYDROXYETHYL CELLULOSE) | $-[C_6H_7O_2-(OCH_2CH_2OH)_3]_n-$ | 294 | $C_6H_7O_2(OH)_3 + 3\left[\begin{array}{c} CH_2-CH_2 \\ \diagdown O \diagup \end{array}\right] \rightarrow [-C_6H_7O_2-(OCH_2CH_2OH)_3]$ |
| CELLULOSE (TRI-) BENZYLATE (ETHER) | $-[C_6H_7O_2-(OCH_2C_6H_5)_3]_n-$ | 432 | $C_6H_7O_2(OH)_3 + 3C_6H_5CH_2Cl + NaOH \rightarrow [-C_6H_7O_2-(OCH_2C_6H_5)_3] + NaCl$ |
| CELLULOSE (TRI-) CYANOETHYLATE (ETHER) | $-[C_6H_7O_2-(OCH_2CH_2CN)_3]_n-$ | 321 | $C_6H_7O_2(OH)_3 + 3CH_2=CHCN + NaOH \rightarrow [-C_6H_7O_2-(OCH_2CH_2CN)_3] + NaOH$ |

TABLE 2. FORMULAS AND BASIC REFERENCE

| HIGH POLYMER | DERIVATIVE OF MONOMER | | |
|---|---|---|---|
| | D.S. = 1 = R | D.S. = 2 = 2R | D.S. = 3 = 3R |
| CELLULOSE NITRATE (ESTER) | $CH_2ONO_2$ ... OH OH | $CH_2ONO_2$ ... $ONO_2$ OH | $CH_2ONO_2$ ... $ONO_2$ $ONO_2$ |
| CELLULOSE ACETATE (ESTER) | $CH_2OC{-}CH_3$ ... OH OH | $CH_2OC{-}CH_3$ ... $CH_2OC{-}CH_3$ OH | $CH_2OCCH_3$ ... $OCCH_3$ $OCCH_3$ |
| CELLULOSE XANTHATE (ESTER) | $CH_2{-}O{-}C{-}SH$ ... OH OH | $CH_2{-}O{-}C{-}SH$ ... $OC{-}SH$ OH | $CH_2{-}O{-}C{-}SH$ ... $O{-}C{=}S$ $O{-}C{-}SH$ |
| CELLULOSE ETHYLATE (ETHER) (ETHYL CELLULOSE) | $CH_2OC_2H_5$ ... OH OH | $CH_2OC_2H_5$ ... $OC_2H_5$ OH | $CH_2OC_2H_5$ ... $OC_2H_5$ $OC_2H_5$ |
| CELLULOSE METHYLATE (ETHER) (METHYL CELLULOSE) | $CH_2OCH_3$ ... OH OH | $CH_2OCH_3$ ... $OCH_3$ OH | $CH_2OCH_3$ ... $OCH_3$ $OCH_3$ |
| CELLULOSE CARBOXY METHYLATE (ETHER) (CMC OR CARBOXYMETHYL CELLULOSE) | $CH_2OCH_2COOH$ ... OH OH | $CH_2OCH_2COOH$ ... $OCH_2COOH$ OH | $CH_2OCH_2COOH$ ... $OCH_2COOH$ $OCH_2COOH$ |
| CELLULOSE HYDROXY ETHYLATE (ETHER) (HYDROXYETHYL CELLULOSE) | $CH_2OCH_2CH_2OH$ ... OH OH | $CH_2OCH_2CH_2OH$ ... $OCH_2CH_2OH$ OH | $CH_2OCH_2CH_2OH$ ... $OCH_2CH_2OH$ $OCH_2CH_2OH$ |
| CELLULOSE BENZYLATE (ETHER) | $CH_2OCH_2C_6H_5$ ... OH OH | $CH_2OCH_2C_6H_5$ ... $OCH_2C_6H_5$ OH | $CH_2OCH_2C_6H_5$ ... $OCH_2C_6H_5$ $OCH_2C_6H_5$ |
| CELLULOSE CYANOETHYLATE (ETHER) | $CH_2OCH_2CH_2CN$ ... OH OH | $CH_2OCH_2CH_2CN$ ... $OCH_2CH_2CN$ OH | $CH_2OCH_2CH_2CN$ ... $OCH_2CH_2CN$ $OCH_2CH_2CN$ |

DATA FOR CELLULOSE ESTERS AND ETHERS.

| THEORETICAL | % OF R GROUP | |
| D.S. = 1 | D.S. = 2 | D.S. = 3 |
| --- | --- | --- |
| R = (-O-NO$_2$-)<br>6.76%N | 2R = (-ONO$_2$)$_2$<br>11.11%N | 3R = (-ONO$_2$)$_3$<br>14.14%N |
| R = (-OCOCH$_3$)<br>21.1% Acetyl<br><br>29.3% Combined<br>HOAc | 2R = (-OCOCH$_3$)$_2$<br>35.0% Acetyl<br><br>48.8% Combined<br>HOAc | 3R = (-OCOCH$_3$)$_3$<br>44.8% Acetyl<br><br>62.5% Combined<br>HOAc |
| R = (OCS$_2$H)<br>% Xanthyl<br>= 36.6 | 2R = (OCS$_2$H)$_2$<br>% Xanthyl<br>= 53.7 | 3R = (OCS$_2$H)$_3$<br>% Xanthyl<br>= 72 |
| R = (-OC$_2$H$_5$)<br><br>23.7% Ethoxyl | 2R = (-OC$_2$H$_5$)$_2$<br><br>41.3% Ethoxyl | 3R (-OC$_2$H$_5$)$_3$<br><br>54.9% Ethoxyl |
| R = (-OCH$_3$)<br><br>17.6%<br>Methoxyl | 2R = (-OCH$_3$)$_2$<br><br>32.6%<br>Methoxyl | 3R = (-OCH$_3$)$_3$<br><br>45.6%<br>Methoxyl |
| R = (-OCH$_2$COOH)<br>34.1% Carboxy-<br>methoxyl | 2R = (-OCH$_2$COOH)$_2$<br><br>54.0% Carboxy-<br>methoxyl | 3R = (-OCH$_2$COOH)$_3$<br><br>67.0% Carboxy-<br>methoxyl |
| R = (-OCH$_2$CH$_3$)<br>% Ethoxyl = 21.6<br>% Ethylene Oxide =<br>21.4; R=(-OCH$_2$CH$_2$)<br>% Hydroxyethoxyl =<br>29.6 R=(-OCH$_2$CH$_2$OH) | 2R = (-OCH$_2$CH$_3$)$_2$<br>% Ethoxyl = 35.9<br>% Ethylene Oxide =<br>35.8; 2R=(-OCH$_2$CH$_2$)$_2$<br>% Hydroxyethoxyl =<br>48.8 R=(-OCH$_2$CH$_2$OH)$_2$ | 3R = (-OCH$_2$CH$_3$)$_3$<br>% Ethoxyl = 45.1<br>% Ethylene Oxide =<br>45.0; 3R=(-OCH$_2$CH$_2$)$_3$<br>% Hydroxyethoxyl =<br>62.3 R=(-OCH$_2$CH$_2$OH)$_3$ |
| R = (-OCH$_2$C$_6$H$_5$)<br>% Phenyl Methoxyl<br>= 42.5 | 2R = (-OCH$_2$C$_6$H$_5$)$_2$<br>% Phenyl Methoxyl<br>= 62.5 | 3R = (-OCH$_2$C$_6$H$_5$)$_3$<br>% Phenyl Methoxyl<br>= 74.3 |
| R = (-OCH$_2$CH$_2$CN)<br>% Cyanoethoxyl<br>= 32.6 | 2R = (-OCH$_2$CH$_2$CN)$_2$<br>% Cyanoethoxyl<br>= 52.2 | 3R = (-OCH$_2$CH$_2$CN)$_3$<br>% Cyanoethoxyl<br>= 65.4 |

of the chemical structures of these derivatives together with pertinent reference data about them.

### Cellulose Ester Derivatives

**Cellulose Nitrate.** The oldest known cellulose derivative, cellulose nitrate, is also the only commercial cellulose ester of an inorganic acid. As guncotton, or as the major ingredient of smokeless powder, the replacement of the available hydroxyl groups in the cellulose is almost complete and the nitrogen content may range from 13 to 14 per cent (theoretical for the trinitrate ester is 14.14 per cent nitrogen). Although the "explosive" type of cellulose nitrate was used in great quantities in World Wars I and II, it has lost some of its military value now that more modern and powerful explosives have been developed.

Cellulose nitrates having lower nitrogen contents (10.6 to 12.5 per cent) continue, however, to be useful in a wide variety of peacetime products: plastic articles, lacquers, enamels, motion picture film (resists curling at high humidities), moistureproofing cellophane, artificial leather, bookbinding cloth, etc.

**Cellulose Acetate.** As a readily moldable plastic and as a lustrous textile fiber, this "acetic acid ester" of cellulose has shown rapid development since its original use as a stiffening coating for the fabrics used in the primitive aircraft of World War I.

Like the nitrate analog, the usefulness and properties of cellulose acetates are influenced greatly by the degree of substitution. For example, cellulose triacetate is soluble in only a few of the common organic solvents (methylene chloride and chloroform, for example) and this limitation has hindered its commercial exploitation. Cellulose triacetate has been used only on a small scale as a textile fiber.

It is in the form of a derivative, having a degree of substitution between 2.3 and 2.7, that cellulose acetate has found extensive use as a textile fiber and as a plastic material. The percentage of combined acetic acid in cellulose acetate plastics usually ranges a little lower (51 to 56) than in cellulose acetate textile fibers (53 to 55.5), whereas cellulose acetate films are made from derivatives having a relatively broad range of degree of substitution (53 to 59).

The commercial popularity of cellulose acetate (D.S. 2.3 to 2.7) stems from its ease of solubility in cheap and common organic solvents (acetone, for example), and its excellent compatability with many plasticizers and resins. However, it generally exhibits poor mechanical properties and sensitivity to moisture, properties that have narrowed its use in the photographic film fields largely to portrait and x-ray types of stationary uses.

Interest in a limited number of mixed cellulose acetate esters has been growing in recent years. Cellulose acetate butyrate and cellulose acetate propionate are the two having the most commercial interest. Plastics made from these mixed esters are tougher, easier to mold because of lower softening points, and exhibit a wider range of solvent and plasticizer compatability than the single component esters.

**Cellulose Xanthate.** Conversion of cellulose to a relatively low substituted xanthate ester constitutes the principal process whereby rayons are manufactured. Unlike the other commercial cellulose esters which retain their composition in the finished product, the xanthate ester is produced only temporarily as a means of making cellulose soluble so that it may then be reshaped in a reconstituted or "regenerated" form. For this reason, the degree of substitution of the xanthate ester is kept low (a D.S. of only about 0.30 out of a possible 3.0) in the interests of economy.

As shown in Table 1, when cellulose is treated with strong caustic soda, alkali cellulose or sodium cellulosate is formed:

$$C_6H_7O_2(OH)_3 + NaOH \rightarrow C_6H_7O_2(OH)_2ONa + H_2O$$

The reaction of sodium cellulosate with carbon bisulfide results in the formation of a low substituted sodium cellulose xanthate ester which is reasonably soluble in caustic soda. In commercial practice the sodium salt of the cellulose xanthate ester is dissolved in NaOH (viscose). Once the viscose solution is forced through tiny holes in spinnerets into an acid spinning bath, it is transformed into solid fine filaments not unlike those made by a spider as it spins its web. The sodium xanthate ester groups are rapidly saponified off and the cellulose is thereby returned to the identical chemical form from which it started, with all the hydroxyl groups in the anhydroglucose monomer units unsubstituted. This "regenerated cellulose" is called viscose rayon.

If the sodium cellulose xanthate solution (viscose) is forced into an acid bath through a thin slot, instead of through a spinneret or thimble with fine holes, a smooth, clear continuous film results. Once again, the sodium salt of the xanthate ester is decomposed, and the resulting purified product in film form is known as cellophane. Chemically, therefore, cellulose in rayon and that in cellophane are identical; the basic difference is that the cellulose in rayons has been shaped into filaments, whereas in cellophane it has been shaped into films.

The importance of the cellulose xanthate ester can best be appreciated, perhaps, by noting that the current annual world production of rayon yarns is about to exceed 4,000,000,000 pounds. Rayons, the most versatile of man-made textile fibers based on cellulose, find applications in ever-widening fields of interest: for example, in woven, knitted, and non-woven fabrics; in all types of apparel from bathing suits to evening gowns; in durable fabric form (e.g., casings for rubber tires and industrial rubber goods of all kinds); in carpets; and in certain types of specialty papers. As one use for rayon is lost to the newer synthetic fibers, entirely new uses for this versatile cellulose-based product evolve.

### Cellulose Ethers

**Cellulose Ethylate (Ethyl Cellulose).** Commercial cellulose ethylates or ethyl celluloses all have a degree of substitution between 2.2 and 2.6. Once again, practical considerations determine the particular degree of substitution for the commercialization of a product. Solubility of ethyl celluloses in organic solvents begins to occur at a D.S. of around 2.0, although greatest solubility in these solvents is exhibited at a D.S. of between 2.2 and 2.6; products having a D.S. from 0.5 to 1.5 are soluble in water or in dilute sodium hydroxide).

Dimensional stability, chemical stability, high strength, good mechanical properties, and excellent moisture resistance are the attributes that make ethyl cellulose ideal for use in plastics and lacquers. Films prepared from lacquer solutions of ethyl cellulose resist moisture and discoloration by sunlight, do not become brittle at low temperatures, and are scuff-resistant. In addition, ethyl cellulose is unaffected by bacteria, insects, or fungi.

**Cellulose Methylate (Methyl Cellulose).** Just as methyl alcohol (the first member of a series of simple alcohols) has unique characteristics, methyl cellulose exhibits properties that set it somewhat apart from the ethyl, propyl, and higher cellulose ethers. It is insoluble in hot water, but soluble in cold water at a degree of substitution of 1.8.

Being odorless, tasteless, and nontoxic, methyl cellulose is an excellent man-made substitute for such natural water-soluble gums as tragacanth and arabic. It is used as a greaseproof coating for paper, and as a thickening agent in the cosmetic, printing ink, and water-soluble paint industries. In recent years, this derivative of cellulose has been finding an increased number of uses in the pharmaceutical field—the most notable being as an appetite depressant. The product swells in the stomach, giving one a "full" feeling even though it has no caloric value.

**Cellulose Carboxymethylate.** This ether, usually sold in the form of sodium carboxymethyl cellulose, or its sodium salt, is commonly called CMC. Once again, the properties of this derivative are closely related to the degree of substitution.

Although methyl cellulose and CMC have parallel properties for some applications, the latter has some advantages. For example, it is equally soluble in hot *or* cold water. It is reasonably stable over a wide range of pH, exhibits wide compatability with many water-soluble materials, and water solutions of it can form excellent films. The property of CMC that makes it so useful is its effectiveness as a stabilizer of colloidal dispersions. It is used as an extender in soaps, a thickener in foods, as a sizing material for textiles, and for many other applications.

**Cellulose Benzylate (Benzyl Cellulose).** Benzyl cellulose ether possesses excellent water insensitivity and good electrical resistance. It is, however, a relatively unimportant derivative and has never been produced in great volume. Its two biggest drawbacks are a low melting point (caused by the bulky benzyl groups holding the cellulose chains apart) and an instability to heat and light. Normally its applications parallel those of ethylcellulose.

**Cellulose Hydroxyethylate (Hydroxyethyl Cellulose or HEC).** This ether has had only a limited success commercially and has not been produced in very large volume. Water-soluble (D.S. = 0.6 to 1.5) and alkali-soluble forms (D.S. = 0.15 to 0.30) are available. The alkali-soluble form has been used mostly as a coating or permanent finish for woven cellulose fabrics such as napkins and bed linens. The uses of water-soluble forms parallel those of CMC and the methylcelluloses.

**Cellulose Cyanoethylate (Cyanoethyl Cellulose).** This derivative, too, is of only minor interest. It hydrolyzes rather easily to carboxyethyl cellulose. Water-soluble and alkali-soluble fibers of this derivative have been made, but only for specialty purposes. The reaction between cellulose and acrylonitrile whereby this derivative is formed is shown in Table 1.

## THE PROTEINS (POLYPEPTIDE POLYMERS)

The proteins are macromolecules of enormous size and complexity. They are unique in that, despite their diversity of composition, the architectural designs of each protein species possess vital specific characteristics. In this sense, proteins may be classed apart from those high polymers that possess little biological activity or direct connection with the life processes. The number and composition of the proteins in the makeup of a living cell, for example, still cannot be established quantitatively.

A still further distinction of proteins from the less specialized high polymers discussed in this textbook is the unique configuration of the polypeptide chain or chains out of which each protein is made. These configurations, ranging from random coils to highly complex helices, are essential to the behavior and role of proteins in the life processes.

Many kinds of naturally occurring amino acids exist, including various types—basic, acidic, neutral, aromatic, sulfur-containing, etc. The formulas of only the major ones will be shown below.

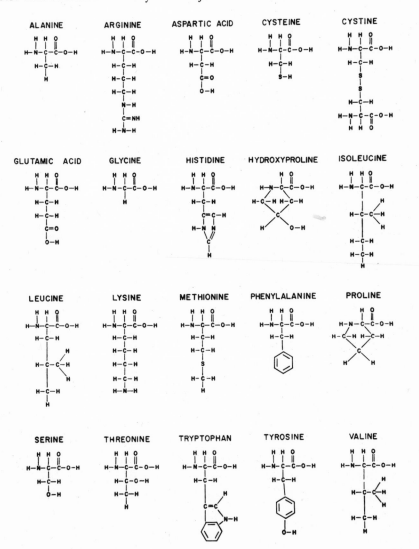

An amino acid is an organic compound containing amino and acid groups—almost without exception it consists of an amino group in a position alpha to a carboxyl group. We might write the prototypic structure of an amino acid as follows:

Just as cellulose macromolecules consist of anhydroglucose units linked together (see Figure 6, p. 16), the proteins are formed from $\alpha$-carboxyl and $\alpha$-amino groups with the loss of water. A typical formula for the backbone of a protein macromolecule may be written as follows:

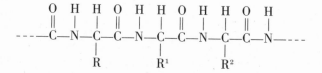

From this formula, it is evident that the repeating unit is an amino acid residue, —NH·CHR·CO—. These residues are joined together by means of peptide linkages, —CONH—, which result from the combination of carbonyl and imino groups. Since the R groups along the chain may vary, it follows that the chemical complexity of protein macromolecules is essentially limitless.

No attempt is made in this text to elaborate on the science of proteins, which is so extensive that it falls beyond the objective of this introductory text. For this reason, we have selected for further discussion only four of the major natural proteins used industrially.

## Wool

Keratin is the principal substance of the wool fiber. Chemically, it is a high polymer fashioned by nature from a wide variety of $\alpha$-amino acids to produce long peptide chains as shown in Figure 8. As may be seen from this formula (also Figure 4, p. 9), wool

```
      SILK                    WOOL
               (SHOWING  CYSTINE  CROSS LINK)
         |                   |              |
         C=O                 N-H            C=O
         |                   |              |
       R-C-H               R-C-H          R-C-H
         |                   |              |
         N-H                 C=O            N-H
         |                   |              |
         C=O                 H-N            C=O
         |                   |              |
       H-C-R               R-C-H          R-C-H
         |                   |              |
         N-H                 C=O            N-H
         |                   |              |
         C=O                 N-H H       H   C=O
         |                   |    |      |    |
       R-C-H             H-C - C-S-S-C - C-R
         |                   |    H      H   |
         N-H                 C=O            N-H
         |                   |              |
         C=O                 N-H            C=O
         |                   |              |
       H-C-R               R-C-H          R-C-H
         |                   |              |
         N-H                 C=O            N-H
         |                   |              |
         C=O                 H-N            C=O
         |                   |              |
       R-C-H               H-C-R          H-C-R
         |                   |              |
         N-H                 C=O            N-H
         |                   |              |
         C=O                 N-H            C=O
         |                   |              |
       H-C-R               R-C-H          R-C-H
         |                   |              |
         N-H                 C=O            N-H
         |                   |              \
         C=O                 H-N
         |                   |
```

Figure 8. Side-by-side comparison of silk and wool molecules.

contains sulfur in the form of cystine built into the main polypeptide chains as cross-links. These cystine linkages are alkali-sensitive.
The process by which moth larvae "eat" wool involves an initial
breakdown of these cross-linkages by means of an alkaline fluid
produced by the larvae, which makes the wool soluble for subsequent digestion.

The resilience or recovery property of wool is, perhaps, its
greatest merit as a textile fiber. Interestingly enough, it is the
periodic presence of these cross-links in wool that accounts largely
for its excellent ability to return to its original state after being
stretched, or its ability to retract or crimp. Silk, which has no cross-

links, does not possess this valuable property to the same extent.

In addition to the cross-linkages through primary bonds by the cystine sulfur atoms, there occurs important interchain hydrogen-bonding (secondary bonds, electrostatic salt-like bridges, intramolecular bonds) between the $C=O$ and NH groups when they fit close to each other in lateral positions along the chain. Such hydrogen-bonding forces come into play also with nylon (see Figures 7 and 13, pp. 17 and 66).

Inasmuch as wool is a natural product, it is not surprising that the proportion of its constituent elements is dependent upon such variables as the terrain and diet upon which the sheep are raised. Nevertheless, an elemental analysis of most purified wool fibers is approximately as follows:

| | | |
|---|---|---|
| Sulfur | 3 | — 4% |
| Nitrogen | 16 | — 17% |
| Carbon | 50 | — 52% |
| Hydrogen | 6.5 | — 7.5% |
| Oxygen | 22 | — 25% |

When wool is hydrolyzed into its constituent amino acids, the main products found are; glutamic acid, leucine, cystine, and arginine.

## Silk

Silk, like wool, is comprised of $\alpha$-amino acids joined together to form long polypeptide chains (see Figure 8). Silk, however, does not contain any sulfur and is therefore free of the cystine cross-bridges so characteristic of wool. Another chemical distinction between wool and silk is that silk is attacked by hydrochloric acid (with attendant decomposition), whereas wool is not. When silk is hydrolyzed to its constituent amino acids, glycine, alanine, serine, and tyrosine are obtained in significant amounts.

## Casein

Casein is the principal protein in milk and the chief component of cheese. It is usually recovered from milk by precipitation with strong mineral acids (HCl or $H_2SO_4$) or enzymes such as rennet; it is formed spontaneously when milk sours.

The simplest basic unit in casein is —NH—CH—CO—. Casein

$$\underset{R}{|}$$

contains only very small amounts of sulfur and phosphorus (about 0.3 per cent). However, casein—as used in the form of plastics and fibers—is cross-linked with formaldehyde to produce a more dimensionally stable product.

The macromolecules in casein—unlike those in the fibrous forms such as wool and silk—are coiled up into macromolecular balls. It is for this reason that casein and most vegetable proteins are commonly called "globular" proteins. In order to produce fibrous materials from globular proteins, it is necessary to uncoil the molecules. Unfortunately, the chemical treatment necessary to bring a globular protein such as casein into solution usually results in a breakdown of the macromolecules. For that reason, fibrous products made from such materials are usually not very strong. The four major amino acids that result when casein is broken down into simpler constituents are leucine, proline, glutamic acid, and lysine.

## Collagen, Gelatin, Leather

Collagen is the chief protein of all soft muscular and connective tissues in vertebrates. When collagen is boiled in water, common *gelatin* results. *Leather,* on the other hand, is normally considered to be a reinforced or stabilized (cross-linked) form of fibrous collagen which resists solubilization by boiling water.

The chemical composition of collagen based on the amounts of the major elements present shows that it is remarkably similar to silk:

| | |
|---|---|
| % C = 49 | % N = 18 |
| % H = 7 | % S = Trace |
| % O = 25 | % P = 0 |

Three main amino acids recoverable from the decomposition products of collagen are glycine, proline, and hydroxyproline.

## CONDENSATION HIGH POLYMERS (C-POLYMERS)

### The Polyamide or Nylon Types

W. H. Carothers, the father of synthetic high polymer science, opened up this tremendous frontier in 1931 with his monumental studies in which he controlled the reaction of dibasic acids and diamines. Aliphatic dibasic acids and diamines are the raw materials used for the manufacture of polyamides.

The first step in the production of the polyamide is the formation of the salt of the diamine and the dibasic acid. The salt is then heated in the absence of air at relatively high temperatures (200–250°C) and the polyamide is formed with the evolution of water.

For the aliphatic series, a single dibasic acid and a single diamine yield a simple linear polyamide which is described by two numbers: the first, the number of carbon atoms in the diamine chain; the second, the number in the acid chain. Thus, polyhexamethylene adipamide, from hexamethylenediamine (1,6-diaminohexane) and adipic acid, is a 6-6 polyamide. This is the popular hosiery-type nylon having the formula $H[N(CH_2)_6NHOC(CH_2)_4CO]_nOH$. On the other hand, polyhexamethylene sebacamide is a 6-10 polyamide. The structural formulas for these two typical linear polyamides may be written as follows:

I. Typical 6-6 Polyamide (Nylon 6,6)

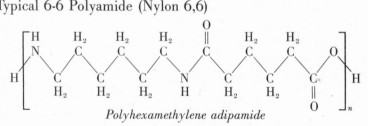

*Polyhexamethylene adipamide*

II. Typical 6-10 Polyamide (Nylon 6,10)

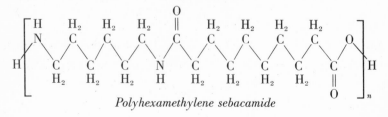

*Polyhexamethylene sebacamide*

The chemistry by which the more common polyamide man-made polymers are produced is shown in Table 3.

## The Polyester or "Dacron" Types

Although W. H. Carothers prepared many of the "self-esterification" types of polyesters, along with his extensive amide research, the typical "Terylene" or "Dacron" polyesters made by condensing glycols and terephthalic acid were not developed until about 1946 by J. R. Whinfield and J. T. Dickson (Brit. Pat. 578,079, and U.S. Pat. 2,465,319).

Since that time, first in Great Britain and later in the United States, the production of polyesters in fiber, film, and resin forms has expanded at a remarkable rate.

Polyesters are usually formed by heating a dibasic acid anhydride with a glycol at high temperatures (200 to 275°C). Table 4 shows the chemical reactions by which the most common or typical polyester polymers are formed.

## ADDITION HIGH POLYMERS (A-POLYMERS)

Most organic compounds contain covalent or "shared" electron bonds. For example methane, one of the basic building blocks of organic chemistry, may be represented as follows:

$$\begin{array}{ccc} \text{H} & & \text{H} \\ \cdot\cdot & & | \\ \text{H} : \text{C} : \text{H} & \text{or} & \text{H—C—H} \\ \cdot\cdot & & | \\ \text{H} & & \text{H} \end{array}$$

In the case of the single bonds represented above, electrons are not really stationary as shown. Rather, they are probably found within a rather large volume of space between the nuclei of the carbon atom and the respective hydrogen atoms, but the electrons do possess an axial symmetry.

In the case of a double bond, however, —C=C— or —C::C—, the presence of the adjacent second pair of electrons destroys the axial symmetry and confines the volume within which the electrons are likely to be found. It has been shown that the second pair of

TABLE 3. CHEMISTRY OF MORE COMMON POLYAMIDE HIGH POLYMERS

| Product | Reaction | General Formula |
|---|---|---|
| Nylon 6 or "Perlon L" | Self-condensation Type $$\begin{array}{c} O=C \\ \diagup \quad \diagdown NH \\ CH_2 \qquad CH_2 \\ \mid \qquad \mid \\ CH_2 \qquad CH_2 \\ \mid \qquad \mid \\ CH_2 \longrightarrow CH_2 \end{array} \quad \left[\begin{array}{c}\text{autoclave}\\ \text{above } 200°C \\ \text{with trace of} \\ H_2O \text{ or catalyst}\end{array}\right] \longrightarrow$$ *ε-Caprolactam* | $-[N(CH_2)_5CO-]_n$ (Nylon 6 from the Lactam of ε-amino caproic acid gives a linear polyamide) |
| Nylon 6-6 or "Perlon T" | Condensation of Diamines and Dibasic Acids $NH_2(CH_2)_6NH_2$ + $COOH(CH_2)_4COOH$ (*Hexamethylenediamine*) (*Adipic Acid*) (Heat 220°C to 270°C in absence of air. $H_2O$ is a by-product of the condensation.) | $-[NH(CH_2)_6NH-CO(CH_2)_4CO-]_n$ (6-6 linear polyamide— *Polyhexamethylene Adipamide*) |
| Nylon 6-10 or "Perlon N" | $NH_2(CH_2)_6NH_2$ + $COOH(CH_2)_8COOH$ (*Hexamethylenediamine*) (*Sebacic Acid*) (Heat 220° to 270°C in absence of air with loss of water.) | $-[NH(CH_2)_6NH-CO(CH_2)_8CO-]_n$ (6-10 linear polyamide— *Polyhexamethylene Sebacamide*) |

electrons in a double bond is held only about half as firmly as the first pair. It is this lack of electron balance or symmetry that leads to the greater chemical reactivity of unsaturated compounds.

A new and important branch of organic chemistry has recently grown up with the discovery and understanding of extremely unbalanced intermediates called "free radicals." A free radical is an intermediate that has an odd number of electrons, or in which one electron is unpaired, for example:

$$H : \overset{\overset{H}{\cdot\cdot}}{\underset{\cdot\cdot}{C}} \cdot$$
$$H$$

Such an intermediate is represented as $R^{\cdot}$ to indicate it is a *free radical*.

Addition or A-polymers result from the polymerization of unsaturated, relatively low molecular weight molecules. A typical general example is:

$$\left[\begin{matrix} CH_2{=}CH \\ | \\ X \end{matrix}\right]_n + R^{\cdot} \rightarrow R{-}CH_2{-}\overset{\cdot}{C}H \xrightarrow{CH_2=CHX} R{-}CH_2{-}CH{-}CH_2{-}\overset{\cdot}{C}H{-}etc.$$
$$\quad\qquad\qquad\qquad\qquad\qquad | \qquad\qquad\qquad\qquad | \qquad\quad |$$
$$\quad\qquad\qquad\qquad\qquad\qquad X \qquad\qquad\qquad\qquad X \qquad\quad X$$

In all cases of addition polymerization, an "active site" must exist in at least one molecular unit. Such "active sites" may arise from any of the following:

1. Upsetting of the couplet balance of electrons to give rise to a *free radical*, as described above. Two common examples of reactions whereby free radicals may be produced for polymerization purposes are as follows:

    (a) $(C_6H_5COO)_2 \xrightarrow{Decomposition} 2C_6H_5^{\cdot} + 2CO_2$
    *Benzoyl peroxide* (*2 free benzyl radicals*)
    or

    (b) $CH_3CH_2CH_2^{\cdot} \xrightarrow{Decomposition} CH_3^{\cdot} + C_2H_4$
    (*free methyl radical*) (*ethylene*)

2. Anionic or cationic mechanisms, usually initiated by acid or base catalysts.

3. Catalysis—acid, base, or photochemical.

TABLE 4. FORMATION OF MORE COMMON POLYESTER HIGH POLYMERS

| Product | Reaction | General Formula |
|---|---|---|
| TYPE I— (Linear) Alkyd Polymers (Simple Alcohol + Polybasic Acids) | Typical Condensation of an Acid with an Alcohol—self esterification type <br><br> $(HO(CH_2)_9COOH) \xrightarrow[-H_2O]{Heat}$ <br> ω-hydroxydecanoic acid | $[-O(CH_2)_9CO-]_n$ |
| TYPE II— Linear | Typical Condensation of Dibasic Acid with a Dihydric Alcohol <br><br> $(CH_2OH)_2 + (CH_2COOH)_2 \xrightarrow[-H_2O]{Heat}$ <br> Ethylene Glycol    Succinic Acid | $[-O(CH_2)_2OCO(CH_2)_2CO-]_n$ |
| TYPE III— Space Network Glyptal Polymers (Glycerol + Polybasic Acids) | Typical Condensation of a Polyhydric Alcohol with a Dibasic Acid <br><br> $CH-(CH_2OH)_2 + 2(CH_2COOH)_2 \xrightarrow[180°C]{Heat}$ <br>   \|<br>  OH     Succinic <br> Glycerol    Acid | $\left[\begin{array}{l}-OCH_2CHCH_2OCO(CH_2)_2CO- \\ \phantom{xxxxxx}OCO(CH_2)_2CO-\end{array}\right]_n$ |
| TYPE IV— Space Network | $CH-(CH_2OH)_2 + RCH=CH(CH_2)_7COOH + C_6H_4(CO_2)O$ <br>  \|<br> OH      Unsaturated Drying    Phthalic Anhydride <br> Glycerol        Oil <br><br> $\xrightarrow[+ \text{ Catalyst}]{\text{Heat}}$ | $\left[\begin{array}{l}-OCH_2CHCH_2OCO(C_6H_4)CO- \\ \phantom{xxxxxx}OCO(CH_2)_7CH=CHR\end{array}\right]_n$ |

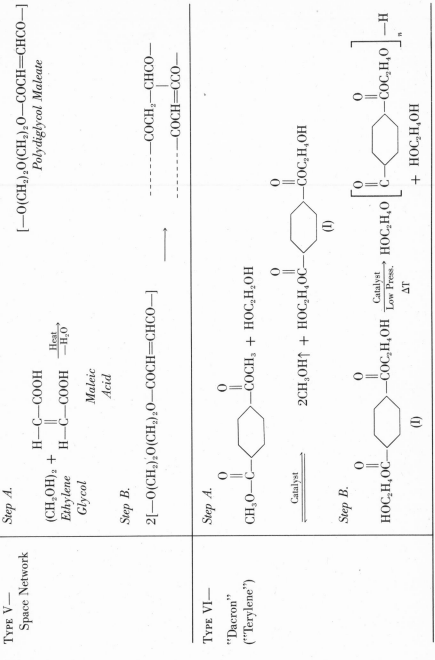

TYPE V—
Space Network

Step A.

$(CH_2OH)_2$ + $\begin{matrix} H-C-COOH \\ \parallel \\ H-C-COOH \end{matrix}$ $\xrightarrow[-H_2O]{Heat}$

Ethylene
Glycol

Maleic
Acid

$[-O(CH_2)_2O(CH_2)_2O-COCH=CHCO-]$
Polydiglycol Maleate

Step B.

$2[-O(CH_2)_2O(CH_2)_2O-COCH=CHCO-]$ $\longrightarrow$

$\begin{matrix} ----COCH_2-CHCO-- \\ \quad\quad\quad\quad | \\ ----COCH=CCO-- \end{matrix}$

TYPE VI—
"Dacron"
("Terylene")

Step A.

$CH_3O-C \overset{O}{=} -\langle \rangle - COCH_3$ + $HOC_2H_2OH$ $\underset{Catalyst}{\rightleftharpoons}$

$2CH_3OH\uparrow$ + $HOC_2H_4OC \overset{O}{=} -\langle \rangle - \overset{O}{=} COC_2H_4OH$

(I)

Step B.

$HOC_2H_4OC \overset{O}{=} -\langle \rangle - COC_2H_4OH$ $\xrightarrow[\Delta T]{\underset{Low\ Press.}{Catalyst}}$

(I)

$HOC_2H_4O \left[ \overset{O}{=} C -\langle \rangle - \overset{O}{=} COC_2H_4O \right]_n -H$ + $HOC_2H_4OH$

The polymerization chain reaction, triggered by any one of the foregoing fundamental mechanisms, results in the "activated" monomer adding initially to another unsaturated monomer, with a transfer of the active site to the end of the resulting dimer; this procedure becomes extended in a very rapid chain-growing manner as follows:

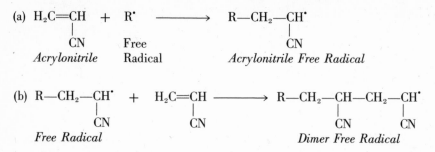

A continuation of the foregoing free radical transmission along the growing chain results, of course, in the formation of highly polymerized acrylonitrile. When a free R' adds to acrylonitrile, however, it may add in either of two ways:

$$(1) \ R' + CH_2{=}CH \longrightarrow R{-}CH_2{-}CH'$$
$$\qquad\qquad\quad |\qquad\qquad\qquad\qquad |$$
$$\qquad\qquad\quad CN\qquad\qquad\qquad\quad CN$$

$$(2) \ R' + CH_2{=}CH \longrightarrow R{-}CH{-}CH_2'$$
$$\qquad\qquad\quad |\qquad\qquad\qquad\qquad |$$
$$\qquad\qquad\quad CN\qquad\qquad\qquad\quad CN$$

If the free radical addition to the monomer occurs exclusively as arrangement (1) or as arrangement (2) (actually the process leading to the more stable configuration is always favored), the so-called *head-to-tail* polymer arises:

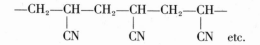

On the other hand, still other possibilities may occur: for example; *head-to-head, tail-to-tail:*

$$-CH_2{-}CH{-}CH{-}CH_2{-}CH_2{-}CH{-}CH{-}CH_2{-}$$
$$\qquad\quad |\quad\ |\qquad\qquad\qquad\ |\quad\ |$$
$$\qquad\quad CN\ CN\qquad\qquad\quad CN\ CN$$

or a *random* arrangement:

$$-CH_2-CH-CH_2-CH-CH_2-CH-CH_2-CH-CH-CH_2-CH_2-CH-CH-CH_2-$$
$$\hspace{1.3cm}\underset{CN}{|}\hspace{1.1cm}\underset{CN}{|}\hspace{1.4cm}\underset{CN}{|}\hspace{1.5cm}\underset{CN}{|}\hspace{0.3cm}\underset{CN}{|}\hspace{2.2cm}\underset{CN}{|}\hspace{0.3cm}\underset{CN}{|}$$

There are four major processes used in high polymer technology to produce substances by addition-type polymerizations. Inasmuch as they are widely used commercially, brief descriptions are included here.

## Emulsion Polymerization

The most important process is that of emulsion polymerization, where the monomer is emulsified in water to which an emulsifying agent has been added. At the end of the polymerization reaction, an emulsion of the polymer is obtained and may be used as an artificial latex for certain technical purposes. The polymer may be coagulated by the addition of acids or salts, or by centrifuging.

## Solution Polymerization

A good example of this process is the polymerization of acrylonitrile in water. If the monomer is soluble but the higher polymer insoluble, the originally homogeneous solution finally separates into a swollen gel and a supernatant liquid. Polymers produced by this process are usually of medium molecular weight.

## Bulk Polymerization

When polymerization occurs in the absence of a diluting medium the entire contents of the vessel gradually polymerizes and forms a solid mass at room temperature. Only those substances which yield a polymer that melts without decomposition are suitable for bulk polymerization on a commercial scale.

## Bead Polymerization

In this process, it is customary to disperse the monomer mechanically in a liquid (usually water) in which it is only very slightly soluble. Each globule of monomer is gradually transformed into a bead of high polymer. Polymerization takes place partly within the droplet (this is the same as bulk polymerization) and partly in the aqueous phase in which the monomer is always soluble to some extent. The polymer which is practically insoluble in water is precipitated onto the droplets and subsequently isolated and purified.

## STEREOREGULAR HIGH POLYMERS

Prior to 1955, the major effort in producing polymers was directed toward changing the chemical composition of the units out of which long-chain molecules are made. Relatively little attention was directed to varying the profile or posture of given polymer chains.

About 1950, Karl Ziegler and his associates* began reporting the use of aluminum organic compounds (e.g., $LiAlH_4$ or $AlH_3$) as catalysts capable of "steering" the polymerization of ethylene, for example, to give macromolecules having stereospecific geometric arrangements of side-groups. These so-called "Ziegler catalysts" were responsible for the subsequent rapid commercialization of low-pressure polyethylenes; they permitted the polymerization to proceed at low temperatures and pressures precluding the necessity of using prior processes which required high pressure equipment. The Ziegler catalysts proved to be effective for the polymerization of vinyl hydrocarbons ($CH_2=CHR$) to macromolecules, but not vinylidene hydrocarbons ($CH_2=CR_1R_2$).

Beginning with a series of "milestone" contributions in 1955, Professor G. Natta of the Polytechnic Institute of Milan further expedited the opening up of this new frontier by investigating new "stereospecific" catalysts capable of controlling the formation and geometrical configuration of macromolecules, including the symmetry of protruding functional side-groups. With this achievement, the application of classic spatial concepts of stereochemistry has progressed rapidly in the field of high polymers.

The principal catalysts advanced by Natta's early research were of two main types:

(1) *Cationic:* Salts of strong acids with weak bases—electrophilic

---

* See *Angewandte Chemie* **64**, 233–9 (1952).

substances; for example, compounds of group II to IV and higher group metals in their highest oxidation state (e.g., $AlCl_3$ and $TiCl_4$, etc.).

(2) *Anionic:* Salts of strong bases or nucleophilic substances; for example, compounds of the lowest oxidation states of group IV to VIII metals (e.g., $TiCl_2$, $VCl_2$, etc.).

The basic idea of stereoregularity was not new. *Trans* and *cis* configurations of organic compounds had long been known. *Cis* and *trans* isomerism is concerned with compounds that are identical with respect to number and kind of constituent atoms, but have different spatial molecular structures. A good example of a *cis* and *trans* isomer is 1-bromo-propene-1.

$$CH_3\!-\!C\!-\!H \qquad\qquad CH_3\!-\!C\!-\!H$$
$$\|\qquad\qquad\qquad\quad\ \|$$
$$H\!-\!C\!-\!Br \qquad\qquad Br\!-\!C\!-\!H$$

(trans form)       (cis form)

Another more common example is:

$$H\!-\!C\!-\!COOH \qquad H\!-\!C\!-\!COOH$$
$$\|\qquad\qquad\qquad\quad \|$$
$$HOOC\!-\!C\!-\!H \qquad H\!-\!C\!-\!COOH$$

fumaric acid (trans)   maleic acid (cis)

It also was known that the *cis* forms could pack or crystallize easily because of their symmetrical molecular posture, whereas the. *trans* configurations were much more difficult to crystallize because of their bulky, less regular chains. A somewhat parallel condition is that wherein stereochemical irregularity or random distribution of groups prevents crystallization. Polyisoprene prepared in such a manner that the methyl groups all lie on the same side of the polymer chain (isotactic type) gives a synthetic rubber that is identical with natural rubber; it crystallizes on stretching and exhibits essentially the same physical characteristics as its natural counterpart. (See p. 63.)

Stereoregular polymers have resulted from the discovery and application of stereospecific catalysts under carefully controlled reaction conditions. Such catalysts serve literally as "Maxwell demons," directing the polymerization reaction along a pre-planned route.

In accordance with the definitions proposed by Natta, the three main types of stereoregular polymers may be illustrated as follows:

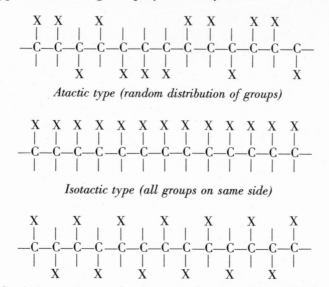

*Atactic type (random distribution of groups)*

*Isotactic type (all groups on same side)*

*Syndiotactic type (regular sequence of groups above and below)*

All three of the foregoing types have been produced and their respective configurations confirmed. Far more complex assemblages are predicted and will no doubt be prepared. For example, following the simple scheme shown above, one might postulate the following more complex stereoregular chain arrangement:

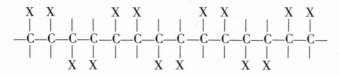

(See also Figure 5)

## NETWORK (THREE-DIMENSIONAL) POLYMERS

Perhaps the simplest way to explain the formation of network polymers is to compare the condensation reactions that occur between ethylene glycol and glycerol, respectively, and succinic acid (see Table 3, p. 36).

When a compound such as ethylene glycol with only 2 reactive side groups, is condensed with a dibasic acid, linear macromolecules are formed. However, when a polyhydric alcohol such as glycerol having more than 2 reactive groups present (3 with glycerol), is condensed with a dibasic acid such as succinic acid, a polymer network structure results, involving primary linkages that build up a three-dimensional architectural structure.

The difference between the linear macromolecule and the network space structure resulting from these reactions, respectively, may be illustrated by the following schematic diagrams:

CASE 1.  Linear Structure—Condensation of Ethylene Glycol (EG) and Succinic Acid (S).

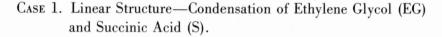

CASE 2.  Space Network (Three-dimensional) Structure—Condensation of Glycerol (G) and Succinic Acid (S).

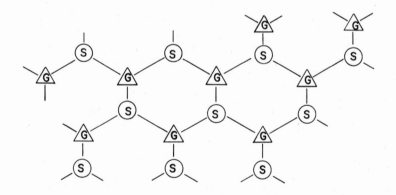

Some typical examples of space network polymer configurations are illustrated in the following pages.

## Cross-linked Cellulose

**Network Structure from Interchain Reaction.** This type of linking, as illustrated in Figure 9, was originally suggested by Hess

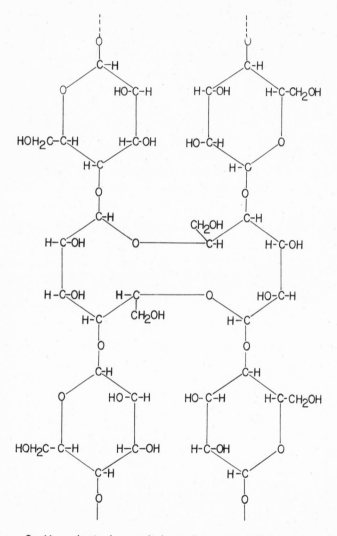

Figure 9. Hypothetical cross-linkage between cellulose molecules, proposed by Hess and Steurer.

and Steurer. They hypothesized (no experimental verification yet has been obtained) that during some stage of cellulose development in the plant, some of the glucopyranose rings of adjacent chains may open and thus furnish the site for the cross-linking of these chains.

The amylene oxide rings (i.e., those connecting carbon atoms 1 and 5 through an oxygen atom) of two opposite anhydroglucose units are opened, and bonding is established between carbon atom 1 of the one unit and carbon atom 5 of the other through the oxygen of the previously closed ring. A second oxygen bond is formed by the same rearrangement between carbon atom 5 of the one unit and carbon atom 1 of the other unit. Thus, a double cross-linkage is established between two adjacent chains.

**Formaldehyde-type Network Linkages.** When formaldehyde is reacted with cellulose under proper conditions of heat and acidity, a product results that is generally assumed, because of its properties, to possess a space network structure. The material becomes brittle and completely insoluble in all known solvents for cellulose. It decomposes before a melting point is reached. Such cross-linking, though still not unequivocally confirmed, is believed to proceed by either or both of the following reactions:

(1)  Between adjacent —OH groups on same anhydroglucose unit.

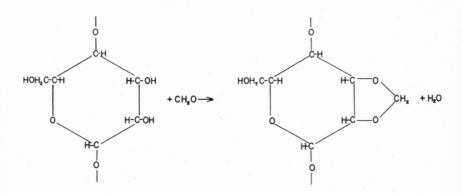

(2) Between —OH Groups on adjacent chains.

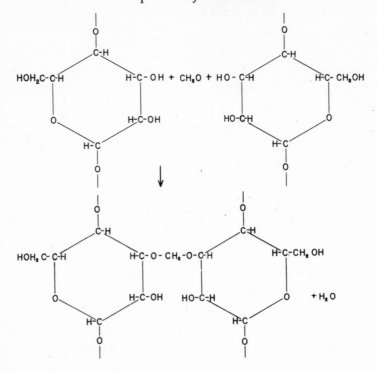

## Network Polyesters

Infusible, insoluble, and very tough network polyester resins result from the direct polymerization of polyfunctional monomers, by between-chain reaction with linear polyester polymers containing unsaturated groups, or by network addition polymerizations sparked by peroxide-type catalysts:

(1) Polyfunctional Monomer:

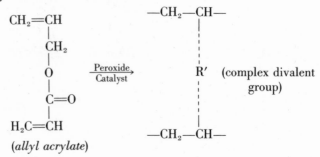

(2) Secondary Reaction with Unsaturated Linear Polymers:

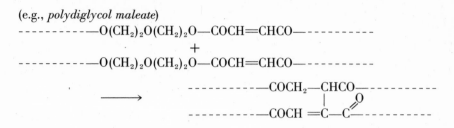

(e.g., *polydiglycol maleate*)

$$- - - - - - - - - -O(CH_2)_2O(CH_2)_2O—COCH=CHCO— - - - - - - - - - -$$
$$+$$
$$- - - - - - - - - -O(CH_2)_2O(CH_2)_2O—COCH=CHCO— - - - - - - - - -$$

$$\longrightarrow$$

$$- - - - - - - - - -COCH_2—CHCO— - - - - - - - - - -$$
$$- - - - - - - - - -COCH=C—C— - - - - - - - - - -$$

(3) Unsaturated Polyester—Bifunctional Monomer Type:

$$
\begin{bmatrix}
—C—CH=CH—CO—O(CH_2)_2O(CH_2)_2—O— \\
\quad\|\\
\quad O \\
\\
+ \\
\\
—C—CH=CH—CO—O(CH_2)_2O(CH_2)_2—O— \\
\quad\|\\
\quad O
\end{bmatrix}
+ (CH_2=CH\phi) \longrightarrow
$$
$$(Styrene)$$

*Polydiglycol fumarate*

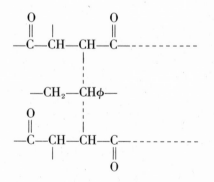

## Network Epoxy Resins

Epoxy resins are prepared from polyethers, usually of low molecular weights, which are cross-linked during a curing treatment to give three-dimensional polymers. The low molecular weight linear molecules contain substituent hydroxyl groups and epoxide terminal groups as in the following example prepared from epichlorhydrin and bisphenol [2,2-bis (4-hydroxyphenyl) propane]:

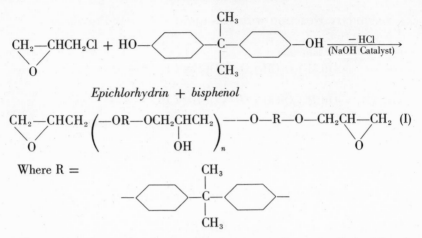

*Epichlorhydrin + bisphenol*

Where R =

The end groups of polymer (I) above may be cross-linked by the addition of a diamine (curing agent) as follows in which two adjacent end groups of polymer (I) are engaged:

$$----CH_2—CH—CH_2$$
$$\diagdown\,O\,\diagup$$

(End Group)

+

$$NH_2C_2H_4—NH—C_2H_4NH_2$$
*(diethylenetriamine)*

+

$$O$$
$$----CH_2—CH—CH_2$$

(End Group)

↓

$$----CH_2—CH—CH_2$$
$$\quad\quad\quad | \quad\quad |$$
$$\quad\quad\quad OH \quad\; NH$$
$$\quad\quad\quad\quad\quad\; |$$
$$\quad\quad\quad\quad\quad\; C_2H_4$$
$$\quad\quad\quad\quad\quad\; |$$
$$\quad\quad\quad\quad\quad\; NH$$     Cross-linked end groups
$$\quad\quad\quad\quad\quad\; |$$
$$\quad\quad\quad\quad\quad\; C_2H_4$$
$$\quad\quad\quad\quad\quad\; |$$
$$\quad\quad\quad\quad\quad\; NH$$
$$\quad\quad\quad\quad\quad\; |$$
$$----CH_2—CH—CH_2$$
$$\quad\quad\quad | $$
$$\quad\quad\quad OH$$

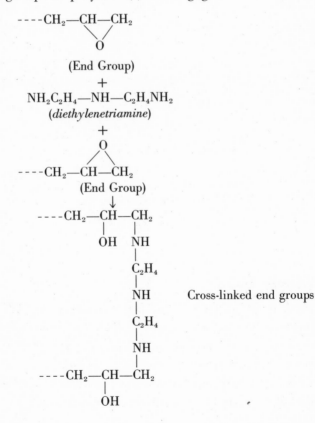

## Network Elastomers (Rubbers)

Polyester elastomers (commonly known as polyurethanes or isocyanate rubbers) possess many properties that make them unique for certain applications. For example, they resist ageing by ozone or ultraviolet light, possess high mechanical abrasion resistance, and are relatively inert to oils and solvents.

Polyurethanes may be prepared by the reaction of a diisocyanate with a glycol as follows:

$$n(\text{HO—R—OH}) + n(\text{OCN—R'—CNO}) \longrightarrow$$

$$\text{HO}\left[\begin{array}{cc} \overset{\text{O}}{\overset{\|}{-\text{R—OCNH—R'—NHCO—}}} \end{array}\right]_{n-1} - \overset{\text{O}}{\overset{\|}{\text{R—OCNH—R'NC}}}{=}\text{O}$$

## Formaldehyde-type Network Resins

Formaldehyde reacts readily with urea, melamine, phenol, or aniline, respectively, to give clear, readily moldable heat-resistant products. These resins find wide application, especially when pigmented to give attractive translucent or opaque molded products: buttons, bottle caps, radio cabinets, tableware, and a host of other products having utilitarian value.

**Urea-formaldehyde Type (Beetle Plastics).** The main component of the three-dimensional network resin is produced as follows:

$$\begin{array}{c} \text{NH}_2 \\ | \\ \text{C}{=}\text{O} \\ | \\ \text{NH}_2 \end{array} \xrightarrow[\substack{\text{(alkaline} \\ \text{catalyst)}}]{+\text{CH}_2\text{O}} \begin{array}{c} \text{NH CH}_2\text{OH} \\ | \\ \text{C}{=}\text{O} \\ | \\ \text{NH}_2 \end{array} \qquad \text{or}$$

*(monomethylol urea)*

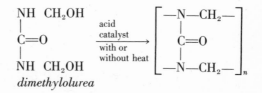

$$\begin{array}{c} \text{NH CH}_2\text{OH} \\ | \\ \text{C}{=}\text{O} \\ | \\ \text{NH CH}_2\text{OH} \end{array} \xrightarrow[\substack{\text{with or} \\ \text{without heat}}]{\substack{\text{acid} \\ \text{catalyst}}} \left[\begin{array}{c} \text{—N—CH}_2\text{—} \\ | \\ \text{C}{=}\text{O} \\ | \\ \text{—N—CH}_2\text{—} \end{array}\right]_n$$

*dimethylolurea*

**Melamine-formaldehyde Type (e.g., "Melmac") Plastics.** Melamine will condense with formaldehyde (using acid or alkaline catalysts) to form methylol melamines. For example, the hexa-methylol compound is known and can be separated as the mono-hydrate, a reasonably stable compound. Intermediate derivatives consisting of the monomethylol, dimethylol and trimethylol mela-mine compounds are more unstable. Insoluble three-dimensional products result when the unstable methylol groups of these inter-mediates react to form methylene linkage between melamine units.

The formation of hexamethylol melamine from melamine by reaction with 6 molecules of formaldehyde is represented as follows:

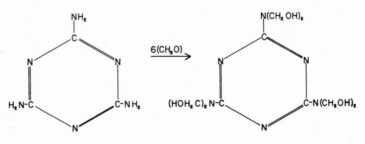

A three-dimensional network structure involving the following type of methylene linkage is believed to be present in a melamine-formaldehyde plastic or resin:

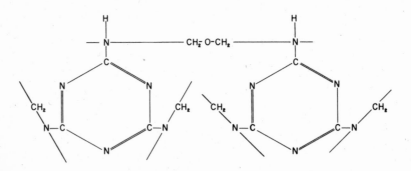

**Phenol-formaldehyde Type ("Bakelite") Plastics.** The chemistry of this polymerization reaction may be written as follows:

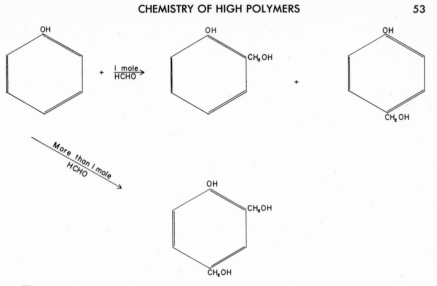

The mono- and dimethylol phenols may then condense with each other to form three-dimensional insoluble space network polymer products.

## THE INORGANIC-TYPE POLYMERS

An understanding of how an element such as carbon can form countless covalent compounds makes it evident that we might expect almost all elements (with the exception of the inert gases which do not possess electron-pair instability) to exhibit some form of polymerizing behavior.

Accordingly, there has been emerging from recent research a growing number of inorganic high polymers paralleling the known organic polymers. Inorganic polymers of the most practical interest are those based on silicon, nitrogen, phosphorus, boron, and a small number of other elements.

It is expected that tin and germanium analogs of the silicones will be heavily researched in the years ahead because of the potential value of such polymers in meeting the needs of our atomic energy and guided missile programs, quite apart from their attractive non-military usefulness.

## Silicones

The covalent capacity of Silicon ($-\overset{|}{\underset{|}{Si}}-$) parallels that of carbon ($-\overset{|}{\underset{|}{C}}-$) so closely that it is logical that its polymer-forming ability has been exploited.

Two basic linkages are involved in the case of silicon-based polymers:

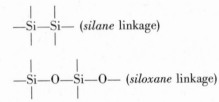

Inasmuch as the silane linkage is unstable beyond a relatively low molecular weight polymer, the "silanes" are not produced in nearly as large a volume as the silicones.

The silicone polymers are based upon chains, rings, and networks of alternate silicon and oxygen atoms. The most common silicone polymers contain methyl and/or phenyl side groups attached to the siloxane chain backbone as follows:

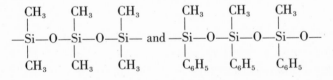

A flow sheet showing how the dimethyl silicone polymers are produced commercially by the General Electric Company is shown in Figure 10.

## Asbestos

This is a unique natural inorganic polymer chemically related to glass inasmuch as it consists of hydrated metal silicates. The remarkable feature of asbestos, the property that gives it wide commercial interest and value, is that it occurs in nature in fibrous form.

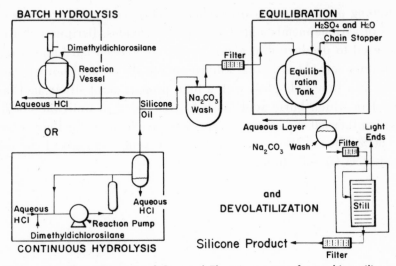

Figure 10. Flow diagram of General Electric process for making silicone polymer products. (*Chemical and Engineering News*)

Normally, asbestos fibers are less than two inches in length, and they can be readily reduced to fragments of much smaller dimensions. Typical formulas for asbestos are:

| | |
|---|---|
| *Chrysotile:* | $Mg_6 \cdot Si_4O_{11} \cdot (OH)_6 \cdot H_2O$ |
| *Amosite:* | $Mg_7(Si_4O_{11})_2(OH)_2$ |
| *Crocidolete:* | $Na_2Fe_5(Si_4O_{11})_2(OH)_2$ |

## Glass

This is, in essence, a space network polymer built up into a three dimensional structure from the following hub component:

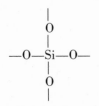

There are more than 50,000 formulas for glass, each involving the contamination or breaking up of the network structure to produce glasses of varying hues and properties. For example, the softening point of glass can be sharply changed by the presence of ions of various metals added originally as oxides. Barium and lead are used to produce flint glass, potassium gives a hard glass, and sodium a soft glass. Pyrex, known chemically as acid borosilicate glass, is a lime-soda glass with a high proportion of silicic acid (as $SiO_2$) in which boric acid (as $B_2O_3$) is added to limit the coefficient of thermal expansion. A representative formula for Pyrex glass is: 80% silica, 12% boron oxide, with varying amounts of sodium oxide ($Na_2O$) and alumina ($Al_2O_3$).

# PART II

# FORMATION OF PRODUCTS
# FROM
# MACROMOLECULES

# 3. The Building Blocks of High Polymers

## MACROMOLECULES TO CRYSTALLITES

Let us picture a long-chain molecule in the simplest possible form as a "matchstick." Then it becomes easier to visualize how such giant molecules can band together and literally "grow" into fibers, films, and other useful products.

For example, if molecular "matchsticks" could be piled together one by one into compact bundles, the resulting bundles would be neatly packed like stacks of lumber in a lumber yard. This would represent the most perfect aggregation of the molecules. If thousands of them should come together or "crystallize" in this manner, fibrils possessing a well-defined architecture would result. On the other hand, if we took a large handful of "matchsticks" and allowed them to fall haphazardly on a table, they would form a jumbled or disorganized pile, lacking symmetry or architectural design. A comparison of these two extremes of association of the same macromolecules is shown in Figure 11.

Now consider a slightly more complex situation involving the intermingling of several "ropes" or sets of molecules, shown in Figure 12. Here we see that one of the macromolecules may wend its way through several regions of high and low order, respectively. This may be observed, for example, by following the paths of molecules (2) and (4) in Figure 12. It is by the packing-together of more and more giant molecules along the schematic lines shown in Figures 11 and 12 that fibrils, fibers, films and other useful products are created.

A most important point to remember about the requisites for creating a high polymer is that the initial *length* of the long chain molecule is of the utmost importance; it must be long enough to produce the continuous structure of a fiber or a film through the

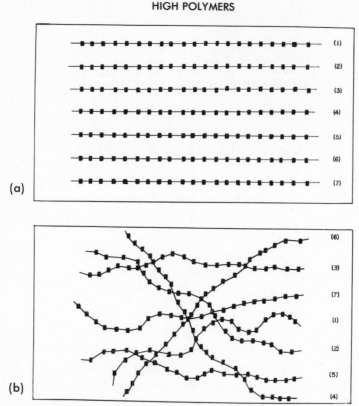

Figure 11. Simplified drawings showing (a) "perfect" and (b) "haphazard" packing of macromolecules.

sequence of steps of progressive aggregation of molecules, interconnection of crystallites, and macroaggregation of such basic building units. It is only when the basic molecule is long enough that one or more segments of it can exist in crystalline areas, while at the same time other segments of the same macromolecule can exist in amorphous or rubber-like areas, that a useful product can be made.

For example, the first "supermolecules" synthesized by Carothers had molecular weights of the order of only 2500 to 5000. They were waxy, weak materials incapable of being formed into fibers. It was not until he synthesized macromolecular materials with molecular weights greater than 15,000 to 25,000 that he achieved distinctly new products. For example, his higher molecular weight

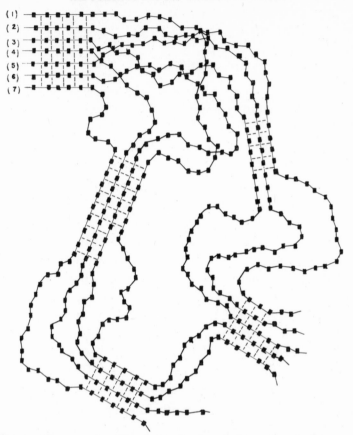

Figure 12. Diagram showing molecules banded together to form ordered nuclei (crystallites):—one molecule may pass through several crystallites connected by disordered areas.

macromolecules ($>$25,000) were tough, opaque solids which melted to give clear liquids at high temperatures. More important, Carothers discovered that fibers could be formed from his new high molecular weight products, fibers which could be stretched, and which were very strong, as strong wet as dry.

A minimum chain length or molecular weight is, therefore, a requisite for each high polymer system to permit the production of a useful fiber or film. The exact magnitude of this minimum molecular weight will vary somewhat for each polymolecular species. A schematic picture of two microfine structures of typical high polymer fibers is shown in Figure 1 (p. 4).

## ARCHITECTURE AND GEOMETRY OF MACROMOLECULES

### Macromolecular Posture or Stiffness

The posture or chain-stiffness of a macromolecule influences significantly the melting point as well as the crystallinity, or the tendency for the molecules to pack in a high polymer. If the macromolecules are stiff like rods, many empty spaces or voids will occur when they are piled haphazardly. On the other hand, if the macromolecules are flexible like string, fewer voids will occur. In other words, chain flexibility plays an important role in determining the amount of space occupied by a giant molecule.

Let us first take a close look at the individual long chain molecules from which some of our most common products are made. In Figures 3, 6, 7, and 8 (pp. 8, 16, 17, 31) schematic models are shown of molecules of polyethylene, nylon, "Dacron," cellulose, silk, wool, and "Vinyon." If atomic models are made of these long chains, significant differences in the inherent mobility and flexibility of the various molecules are evident. For example, the cellulose chain is rigid and can twist or bend to a very limited extent (see Figure 6, p. 16). The silk molecule, on the other hand, is very flexible and can bend or twist easily. Varying differences in molecular "chain-stiffness" are exhibited by the other molecules.

Some molecules have a straight or extended shape, whereas others show a natural tendency to fold. For example, cellulose and silk molecules are normally straight, and while the silk molecule is as *flexible* as that of wool, the latter is resilient and curls.

It is now also recognized that the ease of *rotation* around the primary or "monomer-connecting" bonds, more than the ease of bending or stretching of such bonds, is a major variable in determining the flexibility (or stiffness) of an individual giant molecule. In addition, as will be shown later (see p. 61), when two or more giant molecules become involved, interchain forces and chain flexibility join in fashioning the ultimate architectural pattern of the high polymer.

As a rule, individual macromolecules of the hydrocarbon type such as polystyrene are flexible; they can slip over each other, fold, and bend. Macromolecules of cellulose or cellulose trinitrate are relatively stiff, on the other hand, because only limited rotation around the primary $\beta$-1,4 glycosidic bond is possible (see Figure 6, p. 16); as a result, they behave more like lengths of soft copper wire than like rubber bands. When molecules are rod-like or relatively inflexible, as in cellulose, the most efficient way for them to aggregate is in parallel bundles.

When large groups are attached to the sidearms of macromolecules, they can at times hinder rotation and thereby make the macromolecule more rigid so that certain configurations are stabilized. In the simple case of the isomers of the paraffin-like chains of isoprene, for example, the introduction of one methyl group on the 2 or the 3 position gives natural rubber molecules when the methylene groups are in the *cis* position, gutta-percha when they are in the *trans* position, as follows:

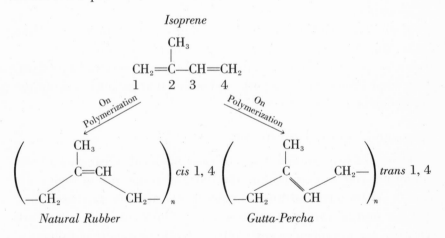

There is still another aspect of macromolecules that sets them apart from the simple prototype monomeric units out of which they are made. For example, the difference between acetic acid ($CH_3COOH$, M.W. = 60.05) and propionic acid ($CH_3CH_2COOH$, M.W. = 74.08) is only one $-CH_2-$ group, yet it makes a difference in physical and chemical properties, as well as an almost 25 per cent increase in molecular weight. On the other hand, a change of one anhydroglucose unit in a cellulose chain of 1500 such monomer units causes a negligible difference in molecular weight (243,162 *vs.* 243,000). Also, the addition of this monomer unit to the cellulose macromolecule does not in any detectable manner change the physical and chemical properties of the latter.

Summarizing the most important characteristics of isolated macromolecules, therefore, we may conclude that the following properties are of extreme fundamental importance in high polymer technology:

1. the stiffness or flexibility of the molecule;
2. its tendency to adopt a straightened-out configuration or a bent, kinked, or coiled shape;
3. the thickness or thinness of the molecule;
4. the length of the molecular chain: long (very high molecular weight), comprised of many monomer units, or short (very low molecular weight), comprised of only a few monomer units;
5. the chemical nature of the side groups that branch out like arms from the backbone or spine of the molecule; and
6. the polymolecular distribution, or the numbers of long, short, and intermediate length molecules that go into making the polymer.

## Interchain Forces of Attraction

There are two characteristics of macromolecules that play a most important role in determining the physical properties of high polymers: (1) the chain stiffness or flexibility already discussed, and (2) the mutual forces of attraction that come into play when two or more macromolecules enter into each other's sphere of influence.

Strong lateral forces of attraction between similar macromolecules will, for example, increase markedly the softening or melting temperature range of a high polymer. On the other hand, when fairly stiff chains are arranged in parallel order, only relatively weak intermolecular forces would be required to achieve a state of three-dimensional order because the stiffer chains permit closer lateral packing. It is therefore quite plausible for relatively stiff chains to possess high melting temperatures accompanied by low heats of fusion—the melting point being related, of course, to the energy necessary to disrupt or spread apart the macromolecules in the areas that are more closely packed.

One might, for example, ask why the softening point of polystyrene is so low. The answer lies largely in the nature or *strength* of the lateral forces of attraction. In general, hydrocarbon-type molecules do not exert exceptionally strong attractive forces on one another. In addition, they are rather flexible and can easily slip along or over each other due to thermal motion. The small potential attractive forces between the chains and the relatively high flexibility of paraffin macromolecules are the two reasons for their low softening temperatures.

Probably one of the clearest ways to appreciate the basic underlying role of interchain forces of attraction in the science of high polymers is to examine what we know about such forces and their relationship to physical properties.

Normal superpolyamides, such as Nylon 66, are solid, tough, high melting point substances. Without chemical modifications, these typical macromolecules may exhibit a wide range of melting points depending on how close the polar groups ($C=O$ and $NH$) can come to each other. For example, if we compare the "perfect" hydrogen-bonding in structure $A$ in Figure 13 with the "imperfect" arrangement of structure $B$, one might predict that the high polymer with structure $A$ might have a melting-point as much as $30°$ to $50°C$ higher than structure $B$, due entirely to the efficiency with which interchain forces come into play.

Drastic changes in properties may be brought about, however, by introducing bulky groups along the chains that can influence hydrogen-bonding even more strongly. This is how the so-called "elastic" polyamides or nylons were predicted and subsequently synthesized.

For example, leaving the polyamide backbone untouched, by replacing the active hydrogen atom in the $—NHCO$ groups with much bulkier alkyl, aralkyl, or alkoxymethyl groups, interchain forces become so weakened that the resulting polyamides become

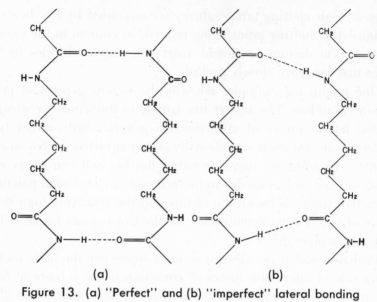

Figure 13. (a) "Perfect" and (b) "imperfect" lateral bonding
between polyamide chains.

soft flexible materials, with a lowered melting point. These are the
polyamide gums and elastomers which have higher solubility in
organic solvents, and a lowered tensile strength and modulus.

A parallel effect is evident in the case of the copolymer of vinyl
acetate and vinyl chloride known as "Vinyon," as shown in Figure
3 (p. 8). Whereas a polyvinylchloride polymer (e.g., "Sarans")
has a high melting point and is tough, introducing relatively small
amounts of vinyl acetate as a copolymer sharply reduces the softening point. This is explained by the presence of the bulky acetate
groups which interfere with the possible hydrogen-bonding; as
shown (see the parallel arrangement of segments of two "Vinyon"
macromolecules in Figure 3), the presence of these side groups prevents close lateral fitting necessary to engage maximum interchain
forces.

Few high polymers exhibit more pronounced interchain forces
of attraction than cellulose. When hydroxyl groups are able to pack
close to each other and in large numbers, as is the case with cellulose (see Figures 6, 7, pp. 16, 17), the interchain forces become so

powerful that the product decomposes before it can melt. Several other groups are capable of exerting similar powerful forces. These are called secondary valence forces, or sometimes Van der Waals' forces, as distinct from primary valence bonds.

Cellulose derivatives such as cellulose nitrate, cellulose acetate, or ethyl cellulose are extremely useful as moldable plastics, because, unlike cellulose, they do have softening points. This is due to the fact that the substituent groups that replace the hydrogen atom on the hydroxyl groups along the chain push the chains apart, weaken the Van der Waals' forces, and cause the molecules to slip and slide, or melt. Figure 14 is a schematic illustration of how the

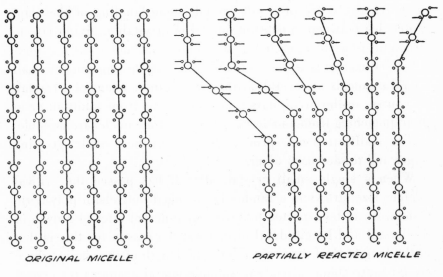

ORIGINAL MICELLE        PARTIALLY REACTED MICELLE

O  GLUCOSE RING
o  OH
∽  SUBSTITUENT

Figure 14. Schematic picture of the initial opening up of a crystallite of cellulose with the formation of a cellulose derivative. [Spurlin, H. M., Trans. Electrochem. Soc., 73, 95 (1938).]

formation of cellulose derivatives causes the chains in cellulose crystallites (regions of maximum interchain forces of attraction) to spread apart.

Interestingly enough, the effectiveness of a partial solvent in swelling cellulose (i.e., in reducing interchain forces) is also related to the size of the molecules that form a solvate with the cellulose chains. For example, in Table 5 is listed a series of swelling agents for cellulose with the best solvent having the largest molecule shown, namely, dibenzyldimethylammonium hydroxide.

## Crystallization and Packing of Macromolecules

When salt or sugar crystals are formed, the molecules are able to pack in perfect order, with the formation of so-called perfect crystals; spacing-defects between the atoms are absent.

As demonstrated in Figures 1 and 3 (pp. 4, 8) it is essentially impossible to produce a high polymer that is perfectly crystalline in the classic sense of a salt crystal; some tangling of the giant molecules between crystalline nuclei is inevitable, giving rise to structural imperfections in terms of regions of molecular disorder.

Crystallization is a process that begins with the engaging of small lateral segments of several chains to form the nucleus of a crystal. Of course, in the precipitation of long chains from solution, or in their quenching from a melt, numerous separate nuclei are possible, and crystallization may proceed by each of these nuclei growing larger and toward each other.

When a single small crystal, after it has passed the critical nucleus size, grows in a randomly arranged long-chain polymeric system, it can be expected to have very different rates of growth in the lateral and longitudinal directions; the reason for this is that in the longitudinal direction (along the length of the chains) there are far more chains already in suitable lateral positions for crystal growth on that crystal face, through the exercising of the interchain or lateral hydrogen-bonding forces.

It is understandable, on the basis of this simplified picture of the crystallization mechanism of macromolecules, that temperature, chain length, size and the protrusion of side groups, etc., will greatly influence the nucleating step and the progress of the crystallization. In addition, it follows that the manner in which the crystallization proceeds controls the ultimate arrangement of the

TABLE 5.   SWELLING AGENTS FOR CELLULOSE

| Compound | Formula |
|---|---|
| Sodium Hydroxide | NaOH |
| Hydrazine | |
| Ethylenediamine | |
| Tetramethylenediamine | |
| Tetramethylammonium hydroxide | |
| Ethyltrimethylammonium hydroxide | |
| Benzyltrimethylammonium hydroxide | |
| Dibenzyldimethylammonium hydroxide | |

molecules and therefore the physical properties of the final product. Furthermore, the size and size-distribution of the full-grown nuclei (or crystallites), their frequency, and their distribution throughout the fine structure network also determine many of the physical and industrial properties of the polymers in the solid state.

Once crystallites are formed, it is usually necessary to melt and/or dissolve the polymer to make them disappear. Quenching of the melt or precipitation of the polymer from solution may then initiate crystallization which gives a *new* internal architectural pattern for the high polymer.

A model illustrating how atoms may pack together to make the beginnings of a perfect "crystallite" or nucleus for crystallization and/or crystal growth is shown in Figure 15. In Figure 16, crystallites are represented as being embedded in a matrix of disorganized chains in a manner somewhat similar to the fine structures depicted in Figure 1, p. 4.

Figure 15. Atomic model showing a perfect crystalline nucleus.
(Courtesy of General Electric Research Laboratory)

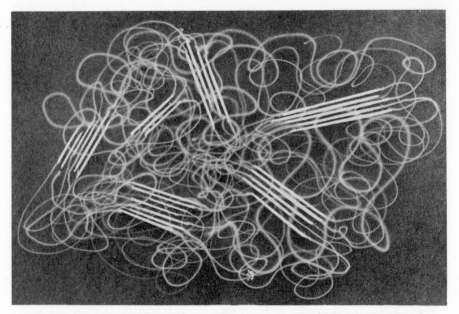

Figure 16. Sketch showing crystalline areas embedded in a matrix of disorganized giant chains. (*General Electric Research Laboratory*)

## Internal Geometry of Macromolecules in High Polymers

The internal geometry (commonly called fine structure) of fibers or films plays a determining role in establishing their ultimate physical and chemical properties, as well as their commercial utility. At this point, it is appropriate to take up rather briefly the crucial steps whereby macromolecules in solution aggregate into basic macro-units upon which depends the physical appearance of high polymers.

In the case of cellulose fibers or films, for example, the size, shape, and orderliness of the crystallite regions play a predominant role as far as such fiber properties as tensile strength, density, rigidity, swelling, and heat-sensitivity are concerned. On the other hand, the less ordered areas and the ratio of such amorphous areas to the crystalline regions are more influential in controlling extensibility and elastic-like behavior.

The art of manufacturing fibers and films having widely different useful properties is based largely on the application of a few key mechanisms that influence the internal geometry of the fibers. Many of these mechanisms, especially the melt-spinning of polymers, find close parallels in the metal industries. A rapid change of temperature—commonly effected by a quenching step—the removal of solvent to precipitate solute, the neutralization of acid or alkaline solvent to cause coagulation—these are the common methods of directing polymer molecules in solution into a preferred molecular architecture.

Fibers exist or may be produced having remarkably wide differences in length, shape, surface properties, and diameter. Macroscopic properties such as these are of considerable importance in determining the ease with which fibers may be fashioned into fabrics or other useful products, as well as influencing the appearance and consumer-appeal of the finished products. Macroproperties, however, can dovetail with molecular properties only within well-defined limits; putting a wool-like crimp into rayon fibers, for instance, is not the simple solution of making rayon more like wool, which possesses a *natural* crimp, a molecular structure that allows wool to relax and return to its original dimension after stretching. With cellulose, on the other hand, the stiffness of the macromolecules and the powerful hydrogen-bonding of the numerous lateral hydroxyl groups prevent these fibers from having good dimensional recovery once they have been stretched to any extent.

Chapter 5 considers in detail methods of measuring the crystallites, and the fine structure of macromolecular aggregations formed when the long-chain molecules go through the transition from the solution to the solid phase.

# 4. Macromolecules in Solution

## MEASUREMENT OF CHAIN LENGTH, OR MOLECULAR WEIGHT, OF MACROMOLECULES

The usefulness of high polymer products is extremely dependent on the average molecular weight (length or degree of polymerization) as well as on the distribution of the *lengths* of the molecules about the average.

It was seen that a minimum molecular weight or "chain length" must be reached before useful fibers or films may be manufactured from macromolecules (p. 60). In this sense, we refer to *average* lengths. However, the amounts of long chains and short chains that are present to give rise to the measured "average" length are important also in determining the ultimate properties and end-use performance of high polymers. For this reason, tremendous effort has been expended during the past quarter of a century in developing methods for measuring the lengths of macromolecules as well as their length distributions.

The various experimental methods for the determination of the molecular weight of macromolecules give, of course, only average values. Fractionation methods, whereby the distribution of lengths about the average may be determined, are described later in this chapter.

In the case of some of these methods (see *Osmometry, End Group* methods that follow), the *number* of molecules in a known mass of materials is counted. Through the use of Avogadro's number ($6.0228 \times 10^{23}$ molecules per mole), a *number-average* molecular weight of the macromolecular substance ($M_n$) can be calculated.

With other procedures, including viscosity and light scattering, the measured effects are a function of the total mass of the component macromolecules. Therefore, heavy molecules (long ones) are favored in the averaging process, and the resulting molecular weight is a *weight-average* molecular weight ($M_w$). In practice, $M_w$ is always equal to or greater than $M_n$.

It is becoming increasingly useful to use the ratio of $M_w/M_n$ as a measure of the chain length distribution (or polymolecularity) of a material. If $M_w/M_n = 1$, it means that a material possesses perfect homogeneity of molecular weight distribution about its average value—a situation that is theoretically possible, but most unlikely to be encountered in practice. The greater the deviation of the ratio from 1, the more heterogeneous is the chain length distribution of the high polymer.

## Solution Viscosity as Related to Molecular Chain Length

Even prior to 1930, Professor Hermann Staudinger proposed that macromolecules (he did not recognize them then in the same sense that our modern technology does) showed in some instances phenomenal increases in viscosity with increases in concentration when dissolved in a solvent. For example, a 1 per cent solution of sucrose in water increases its viscosity to a negligible extent; on the other hand, a 1 per cent solution of cellulose nitrate ester in acetone causes a fifteen- or twenty-fold increase in viscosity.

Staudinger visualized molecules of cellulose nitrate, for example, as relatively rigid rods in solution. These molecular rods exhibited Brownian motion and the very high viscosities observed were explained by their extremely high molecular volume, schematically represented as the volume of a sphere, the diameter of which was equal to the length of the rod-like molecules. As the length of the molecule increases, the corresponding molecular volume grows rapidly, paralleling an equally rapid increase in the viscosity as illustrated in Figures 17, 18, and 19.

With his work to develop a quantitative relationship between the solution viscosity of macromolecules and molecular weight, Staudinger was the first to point out, on empirical grounds, the approximate proportionality between reduced viscosity, $\eta_{sp}/c$, and molecular weight. Proportionality is more closely observed when intrinsic

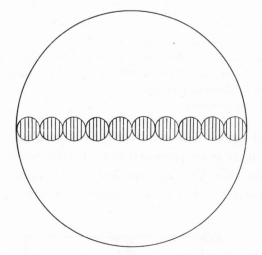

MAXIMUM HYDRODYNAMIC VOLUME OF 10 MOLECULES IN SOLUTION
HAVING A D.P.= 10 EACH.
AGGREGATE DEGREE OF POLYMERIZATION = 100.

COMPARISON OF MAXIMUM HYDRODYNAMIC VOLUME OF A SINGLE MOLECULE
IN SOLUTION WITH A D.P. = 100 Vs 10 MOLECULES HAVING AN AGGREGATE
D.P. = 100

Figure 17. Two-dimensional illustration comparing the hydrodynamic volumes of short- and long-chain molecules, respectively, demonstrating the role of chain length on solution viscosity.

viscosity, $[\eta]$, the limiting value of reduced viscosity at zero concentration, is used to minimize concentration effects. The intrinsic viscosity, $[\eta]$, of a high polymer, defined as $\lim\limits_{c \to 0} \dfrac{\eta_{sp}}{c}$ has come to be regarded as a fundamental characteristic of the material, directly related to the degree of polymerization (D.P.) and thereby to other significant properties. Since the extrapolated values of the relative viscosity-concentration curve $d\eta_r/dc$ at zero concentration is identical with the limiting values of $\eta_{sp}/c$ and $(\ln\eta_r)/c$, the intrinsic viscosity may be approximately equated as follows:

$$[\eta] \equiv \lim_{c \to 0} \frac{\eta_{sp}}{c} \equiv \lim_{c \to 0} \frac{\ln\eta_r}{c}$$

Staudinger's original empirical equation was:

$$\left(\frac{\eta_{soln.} - \eta_{solv.}}{\eta_{solv.}}\right) = \eta_{sp}/c = K_m M \quad \ldots \ldots \quad (1)$$

Where:   $\eta_{soln.}$ = viscosity in cps. of solution at low concentration
$\eta_{solv.}$ = viscosity in cps. of solvent
$\eta_{sp}$ = specific viscosity [a ratio as defined in equation (1)]
$c$ = conc. in gm per deciliter (as originally proposed)
$M$ = molecular weight
$K_m$ = constant

Recently it has been shown that, for many polymers in solution, intrinsic viscosity is proportional to molecular weight or degree of polymerization raised to an exponent $a$, the value of which lies between 0.5 and 1.0. For most solutions of cellulose and cellulose

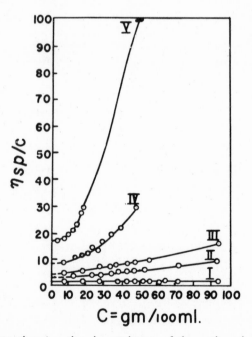

Figure 18. Data showing the dependence of the reduced viscosity ($\eta_{sp}/c$) on concentration at a series of D.P. levels (ordinary graph paper plot).

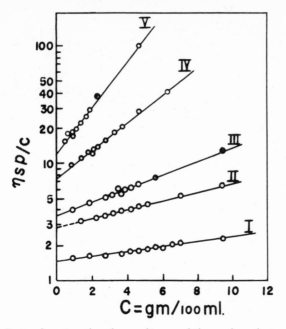

Figure 19. Data showing the dependence of the reduced viscosity ($\eta_{sp}/c$) on concentration at a series of D.P. levels (semilogarithmic graph paper plot).

derivatives, the value for $a$ is very nearly 1, so that simple proportionality holds to a reasonable degree. However, significant deviations from 1 do occur with other macromolecular systems in which the molecules are not as stiff or as fully extended in solution as are cellulose and most cellulose derivative macromolecules ($a = 0.5$ to 1), or in which the molecules behave more like rigid rods ($a = 1$ to 2). Today, Staudinger's original viscosity-molecular weight relationship is almost universally expressed as follows:

$$(\eta_{sp}/c)_{c \to 0} = [\eta] = K_m M^a \quad \ldots \ldots \quad (2)$$

Where $c = $ conc. gm/100 ml

Equation (2) incorporates two important improvements over equation (1).

1. The specific viscosity ($\eta_{sp}$) has been replaced by the intrinsic viscosity $[\eta]$ already defined (a term introduced by E. O. Kraemer in 1938).
2. The value of $a$ in equation (2) may vary between 0.5 and 2.0.

The constants $K_m$ and $a$ respectively, of equation (2) are characteristic for a given species of macromolecule. They must, however, be established for each species by means of an "absolute" method of measuring molecular weight, such as osmometry, or light scattering procedures which are described in the following pages.

Because the intrinsic viscosity $[\eta]$ is easier to interpret theoretically, and permits a more reliable comparison of viscosity data at different concentrations, it is now almost universally used. However, the determination of several viscosities on each sample, followed by the necessary graphic plotting of $\eta_{sp}/c$ vs. $c$ and subsequent extrapolation to $c = 0$ is burdensome. Accordingly, many mathematical relationships have been devised to make it possible to calculate the intrinsic viscosity from a single viscosity measurement at a relatively high concentration, where solution viscosities may be reliably measured.

One of the more commonly used mathematical expressions for calculating intrinsic viscosities from a single solution viscosity measurement at a finite concentration is the modification of the original Huggins equation proposed by Martin: *Original Huggins Equation* [Huggins, M. L., *J. Am. Chem. Soc.*, **64**, 2716 (1942)]:

$$\eta_{sp}/c = [\eta] + K'[\eta]^2 c + \quad . \quad . \quad . \quad . \quad . \quad .$$

Modification proposed by Martin [Martin, A. F., Am. Chem. Soc. Meeting, Memphis, (Apr. 20–24, 1942)]:

$$\log \eta_{sp}/c = \log [\eta] + K[\eta]c$$

In applying the Martin equation to a given set of data, the concentration should be expressed in gm/100 ml. However, since the rate of increase in density with concentration usually is very small, the use of concentration in gm/100 gm will result in a relatively small error, usually within the experimental limits of measurement.

In Table 6 is assembled a list of typical intrinsic viscosity data for some of the more common species of high polymers, together with generally accepted corresponding degree of polymerization data.

Conversion of viscosity data to basic degree of polymerization values is done in order to establish a convenient reference for

TABLE 6.  TYPICAL INTRINSIC VISCOSITY [$\eta$] AND DEGREE OF POLYMERIZATION
DATA FOR COMMON MACROMOLECULES

| Commercial High Polymer Molecule | [$\eta$] | Generally Accepted D.P. Range |
|---|---|---|
| Raw cotton cellulose | 18–25 | 3600–5000 |
| Absorbent cotton linters | 10 | 2000 |
| Acetate grade wood pulp | 7 | 1400 |
| Typical viscose grade wood pulps | 5 | 1000 |
| Cellophane wood pulps | 3.5 | 700 |
| Viscose rayons | 2–3 | 400–600 |
| Cellulose acetate rayons | 1.5–2.0 | 300–400 |
| Level off D.P. hydrocelluloses from wood pulps | .75–1.0 | 150–200 |
| from rayons | .10–.30 | 20–60 |
| Commercial cellulose nitrates | 0.65–13 | 65–1300 |
| Sheet rubber | 9 | 500–1000 |
| Tobacco mosaic virus* | 0.6–1.00 | — |

* There is some disagreement on a true [$\eta$] value for Tobacco Mosaic virus. Some workers believe it
may be much higher than the range shown above.

noting relative changes in the average degree of polymerization of
high polymers. The basic degree of polymerization is used in lieu
of measured units such as the viscosity in centipoises or the fluidity
in rhes, because it serves as a more effective way of describing
changes accompanying the degradation of cellulose and cellulose
derivatives. Furthermore, it specifies the precise procedure by
which such data are obtained and calculated.

Unfortunately there do not exist universally accepted absolute
methods for expressing the molecular weight (or D.P.) of high
polymers, or even of one species such as cellulose and cellulose
derivatives. Nevertheless, it is a great convenience to use a *uniform*
degree of polymerization scale.

A recommended procedure for the measurement of the basic
degree of polymerization of cellulose and cellulose derivatives has
been described in the literature.* This method is particularly ap-

* *Ind. Eng. Chem.*, Anal. Ed. **16**, 351–44 (1944); *Ind. Eng. Chem.*, **44**, 893–96 (1952); *Ind. Eng.
Chem.*, **48**, 333–335 (1956).

plicable to commercial cellulose products in which the D.P. levels are below 3000, and preferably below 2000. Although it specifies that viscometers should be selected in such a manner that flow times in all cases are kept at approximately 100 sec or greater, to keep the kinetic energy corrections at a very low value, the method does not allow for adjusting the velocity gradient to a uniform value. There is, therefore, some arbitrariness about the conversion of the intrinsic viscosity data to basic D.P. values.

This method does, however, permit the calculation of an intrinsic viscosity value $[\eta]$ for cellulose from a single viscosity measurement at 0.5 per cent concentration. It then allows for the conversion of the "calculated intrinsic viscosity" to a basic D.P. value using equation (2) above wherein $K^m = 260$ when the solvent is cuprammonium hydroxide, or $K^m = 190$ when the solvent is cupriethylenediamine. The degree of polymerization data listed in Tables 6, 7, 8 and 9 for cellulose and cellulose derivatives all were obtained using this basic D.P. scale.

## Osmometry for the Measurement of Molecular Weight

Next to the viscosity method, procedures involving the measurement of osmotic pressures are the most commonly used for determining the molecular weight of macromolecules. Unlike the viscosity method, which gives a reasonably close value for the *weight-average* molecular weight $(M_w)$, the osmotic pressure method gives a *number-average* value $(M_n)$.

The osmotic pressure of a solution may be determined by:

1. *The static-elevation method.* This involves the measurement of the liquid head developed by the influx of solvent into the solution through a suitable semipermeable membrane, resulting from osmotic forces caused by the difference in the activities of the solvent molecules in the two phases.

2. *The dynamic-equilibrium method.* In this case, the externally applied pressure necessary to counterbalance the osmotic pressure is determined.

In the determination of molecular weight by the osmotic pressure method, we are concerned with the total weight of polymer dissolved in a given volume and also with the *number* of particles contained in this volume. The law expressing the proportionality between osmotic pressure and the number of molecular particles was first expressed by van't Hoff as follows:

$$M_n = \frac{RT}{(\pi/c)}$$

When this equation is applied to high polymer solutions, it must be used in the following form:

$$(\pi/c)_{c=0} = RT/M_n$$

Where $\frac{\pi}{c}$ = reduced osmotic pressure

$\quad \pi$ = osmotic pressure of solution
$\quad c$ = conc. by weight of solute per unit volume
$\quad R$ = gas constant expressed in appropriate units
$\quad T$ = absolute temperature
$\quad M_n$ = number average molecular weight of the solute

In very dilute solutions, the osmotic pressure depends on the *number* of macromolecules, irrespective of their size. Therefore, in making the molecular weight calculation, the total *weight* of all the particles is divided by their *number* to obtain the average molecular weight. It is true, strictly speaking, that the proportionality between the number of particles and the osmotic pressure will hold only at infinite dilution since the above equation becomes identical with that of van't Hoff when $c = 0$. At finite concentrations for simple molecules, deviations will occur which, in the region of measurable pressures, are small only in the case of compounds of low molecular weight, or of systems with large compact molecules. In the case of macromolecules, deviations appear even at the lowest concentrations which can be used to obtain a measurable pressure.

In making measurements of the osmotic pressure of solutions of polymeric mixtures, it is customary to plot $(\pi/c)$ vs. $c$, and obtain the value of $(\pi/c)$ at $c = 0$ by extrapolation to infinite dilution. When this is done, the number-average molecular weight is defined by:

$$M_n = \frac{1}{\Sigma f_x / M_x}$$

Where $f_x$ is the *fractional* weight of the xth species in the mixture, and $M_x$ is the *molecular* weight.

It is important to remember that the osmotic pressure method for determining number-average molecular weight is sensitive to the presence of short molecules, whereas long molecules have a relatively minor influence.

Essentially, a *static* osmometer is an apparatus capable of holding a solution of a polymer in one compartment that is separated by a membrane from a second compartment containing the same solvent in which the polymer is dissolved. The membrane should be permeable only to the solvent. A connection is usually made to a capillary above the compartments to permit the osmotic pressure to be balanced by a hydrostatic pressure. Membranes usually consist of porous glass or metal discs, or of films of regenerated cellulose, gelatin, or rubber.

A *dynamic* osmometer, on the other hand, is simply one in which an external pressure is applied to *prevent* osmosis.

## Light Scattering

When light enters a colorless suspension of particles, it is scattered if the refractive index of the particles differs from that of the medium in which they are suspended because of nonhomogeneous molecular structure. If the particles are optically isotropic, spherical, and small in diameter as compared to the wave length of the light, the light that is scattered at $90°$ to the incident beam is completely polarized. It is because of light scattering, for example, that some colloidal dispersions exhibit the *Tyndall Effect* (opalescence), and the sky appears light and blue (*Rayleigh scattering*). For true light scattering to occur, the wave length of the light should not be changed in the process.

Many dissolved molecules will scatter light because they are only a few hundred Angstrom units (A) in size and are, therefore, small in comparison to the wave length of visible light (3900A–7000A). A relationship has been found between the sum total of the light-scattering powers of the individual macromolecules in solution and the angles through which the light is scattered.

Light-scattering data give a molecular weight value that is a weight-average value ($M_w$). For example, in the case of particles that are smaller than 1/20 to 1/10 of the incident wave length, it is usually possible to measure only the molecular weight by the light-scattering technique. However, when the particles are larger than this value information may be obtained about their shapes, i.e., whether they are spheres, rods, or coils. In characterizing the shapes of molecules in solution, it is necessary to measure the entire light-scattering envelope and then extrapolate the data to zero angle and zero concentration.

Accurate determinations of the molecular weights of high polymers by thermodynamic methods require appropriate extrapolation to infinite dilution from measurements made at finite concentrations. As was shown in the case of the osmotic method, it is customary for this purpose to plot the ratio of the osmotic pressure to the concentration, ($\pi/c$) vs. $c$. Light-scattering measurements are usually handled in an equivalent manner by plotting $\left(\dfrac{Hc}{\tau}\right)$ vs. $c$, which almost always gives a straight line.

The weight-average molecular weight ($M_w$) is then determined, using the following equation:

$$\left(\frac{Hc}{\tau}\right)_{c=0} = \frac{1}{M_w}$$

where $\tau$ = absolute turbidity in excess of the turbidity of the solvent
   $c$ = conc. in gm/cc

$$\left(\frac{Hc}{\tau}\right) = \frac{1}{M_w} + 2Bc$$

where $B$ = second virial coefficient

$$H = [32\pi^3\eta_0{}^2(\eta - \eta_0)^2/c^2]/3\lambda^4 N$$

where $\eta_0$ = refractive index of solvent
   $\eta$ = refractive index of solution
   $\lambda$ = wave length of incident light
   $N$ = Avogadro's number

Accurate measurements of the molecular weight and/or particle shape of high polymers by light-scattering techniques may be hindered by the presence of dust particles or small quantities of coarser particles. The suspensions examined must therefore be carefully freed from coarser particles by centrifuging or filtration.

### Ultracentrifuge Methods (Sedimentation Equilibrium)

The use of the ultracentrifuge to give weight-average molecular weights of polymers has been limited in scope because it entails very elaborate techniques and the use of costly equipment. In addition, the basic requirements for the application of the procedure are rather severe:

(1) Solution of the polymer must be stable for long periods of time, sometimes weeks.
(2) There must be a difference in refractive index and density between the solvent and polymer.
(3) The polymer must be soluble at or near room temperature.
(4) The solvent must have a relatively low viscosity.

Nevertheless, the ultracentrifuge still provides one of the most generally applicable methods for determining the molecular weight of highly polymerized substances, and in addition has the advantage of giving information about the polydispersity or molecular chain length distribution of high polymers. Light-scattering methods also are of great value and widely used.

There are two ways that sedimentation rates with an ultra-centrifuge can be used to measure the molecular weight of high polymers. Both depend on the fact that during centrifuging, macromolecules in solution migrate outwards in the centrifugal field while Brownian motion encourages diffusion in the opposite direction. In either case, the macromolecules are forced to move against internal frictional forces.

**The Equilibrium Method.** This procedure involves running the ultracentrifuge at a steady slow speed for a long period of time— sometimes as long as one or two weeks. Ultimately a thermodynamic equilibrium is reached in which the polymer molecules are suspended within the cell on a chain length or molecular weight basis, the longest molecules being at the bottom end of the cell and the shortest ones at the top. The following formula is used to calculate a weight-average molecular weight by this method:

$$M_w = \frac{2RT \log \varepsilon (C_2/C_1)}{(1 - V\rho)\omega^2(X_2^2 - X_1^2)}$$

Where $R$ = Gas constant

$T$ = Absolute temperature

$(1 - V\rho)$ = A buoyancy factor in which $V$ is the partial specific volume of the polymer, and $\rho$ is the density of the solution

$\omega$ = Angular velocity of rotation

$C_1$, $C_2$ = Weight concentration of polymer at two points, $X_1$ and $X_2$, respectively, in the ultracentrifuge cell corresponding to radii of rotation

**The Rate Method.** With this method, concentration is a critical variable because it is essentially upon this that the *rate* of sedimentation depends. Extrapolation of data to infinite dilution is necessary and the experiments must be run at very low concentrations. The basis of the procedure lies in making equal the centrifugal forces and the frictional forces acting on a particle of mass $m$. Experimentally, it differs from the equilibrium method in that the sedimentation *velocity* of the molecules in solution is measured, with the ultracentrifuge running for only 2 to 3 hours in very high centrifugal field, around 200,000 G.

It is necessary with this method to measure the diffusion constant $D$ (which, like the sedimentation rate, is related to frictional forces). A measure of the diffusion rate is usually obtained by the use of a separate stationary chamber wherein pure solvent is placed above the polymer solution and the progressive blurring of the separating boundary occurs as the polymer molecules diffuse upwards into the supernatant solvent.

The following equation is used to calculate weight-average molecular weights, and two sets of measurements are required.

$$M = \frac{RT}{(1 - V\rho)} \frac{S}{D}$$

Where $R$, $T$ and $(1 - V\rho)$ are as before,

$S$ = Sedimentation Constant = $\dfrac{\text{Velocity of sedimentation}}{\text{Intensity of centrifugal field}}$

$D$ = Diffusion Constant

The extrapolation of $S$ to infinite dilution is obtained by plotting $\left(\dfrac{1}{S}\right)_{c\to 0}$ vs. $C$. It is now common to designate $\left(\dfrac{1}{S}\right)_{c\to 0}$ as $\dfrac{1}{S_0}$.

## End Group or Chemical Method

When a giant molecule is linear and contains an "end" or terminal group (see Figures 2, 6, pp. 7, 16) that is unique and
capable of reaction, a true number-average molecular weight can
be obtained in certain cases, at least. This chemical method for
measuring the molecular weight of polymer molecules (chemical
analysis of the number of specific functional end groups, see below)
loses sensitivity as the length of the molecules increases, so that it
falls down in many cases in molecular weight ranges that have the
most commercial value and interest. For example, when the degree
of polymerization is greater than 75 to 100, the number of end
groups becomes so small *in proportion* to the total weight of the
polymer, that analytical methods are generally not sensitive enough
to detect these end groups with sufficient accuracy to permit the calculation of a reliable molecular weight. Nevertheless, the method
does find usefulness for relatively low molecular weight polymers,
and the following is a listing of some of the specific areas in which
it is used:

(1) Nylon 66 H—[NH·$(CH_2)_6$NH—CO·$(CH_2)_4$·CO—]$_n$ OH.
This linear molecule should contain only one active —$NH_2$
group and one active —COOH group. These groups are
readily measurable, and from their amounts, number-average molecular weights for nylon 66 may be determined.
(2) Highly degraded celluloses (D.P. = 20 to 50), where the
number of potential aldehyde groups may be measured.
(3) Vinyl polymerizations where specific end groups result from
chain transfer reactions.

## Boiling Point Elevation (Ebullioscopic) Method

There are two classic methods for measuring the *number* of simple molecules in solution—the lowering of vapor pressure and of
freezing point, respectively. These methods are based on the

activity of a solute dissolved in a solvent, which is proportional to its mole fraction as the concentration of the solute gets small enough; the activity of the solvent must also equal its mole fraction under these conditions, so we can conclude that the *depression* of activity of a solvent by a solute is related to the mole fraction of the *solute*. This depression of activity is what accounts for vapor pressure lowering (boiling point elevation) and/or freezing point lowering.

Unfortunately, in the case of macromolecules in solution, only small differences in temperature result, at times only $.001°C$. Pending the use of a new dimension in the sensitivity of temperature measurement, boiling point elevation methods are bound to have only limited applicability for high polymers, and then mostly for relatively low molecular weight species.

The ebullioscopic or boiling point elevation method involves the measurement of the temperature differential $\Delta T$ required to return the vapor pressure to its equilibrium value at the boiling point of the pure solvent. With this method the following formula is used:

$$(\Delta T_b/c)_{c=0} = \frac{\left(\frac{RT^2}{\rho\Delta H_v}\right)}{M_n}$$

Where $\rho$ = density of solvent

$\Delta H_v$ = latent heat of vaporization of solvent per gram

$c$ = conc. of the solution in gm per cc

$R$ = gas constant

$T$ = absolute temperature

### Freezing Point Depression (Cryoscopic) Method

In this case, a measurement is made of the temperature-lowering differential $(\Delta T_f)$ necessary to make the activity of the solvent in the solution equal to its activity in the pure state at its freezing point. The classic formula used then is:

$$(\Delta T_f/c)_{c=0} = -\frac{\left(\frac{RT^2}{\rho\Delta H_f}\right)}{M_n}$$

## Direct Photographic Method—Electron Microscopy

The method of direct measurement of the lengths of giant molecules by electron microscopy has received little attention to date, but it should and will no doubt be investigated exhaustively in the future.

Conceivably, if giant molecules could be de-aggregated by some means—such as ultrasonic vibrations—into bundles of molecules consisting at most of a few chains each, and if highly magnified pictures of these molecules could be made with an electron microscope, direct and essentially absolute molecular weights might be obtained.

One preliminary attempt to do this using low D.P. hydrocelluloses has provided interesting data. At best, however, the data shown in Table 7 should point only to the need and the promise of further work using this direct approach to the measurement of the molecular weight of linear molecules that are well-packed and capable of lateral separation into component entities.

In the work reported in Table 7, attention is called to the remarkable agreement between viscosity average molecular weights (or D.P.) obtained by intrinsic viscosity measurements, and the corresponding values for these samples obtained by using a pretreatment of the same samples with ultrasonics, subsequent palladium shadowing, and taking direct electron microphotographs of the reduced aggregates (see frontispiece).

## POLYMOLECULARITY OR CHAIN LENGTH DISTRIBUTION

High polymers, both natural and man-made, are not homogeneous materials. Each species consists of macromolecules of varying lengths, which means that an average molecular weight has limited value for the characterization of a high polymer; the distribution of molecular sizes about the average, or the molecular chain length uniformity of a high polymer, are important. Many mechanical and physical properties of high polymers depend upon the nature of

TABLE 7. RELATION BETWEEN CUOXAM VISCOSITY-DEGREE OF POLYMERIZATION AND PARTICLE LENGTH VIA ELECTRON MICROSCOPE *

| Sample | Method | Swelling Time, 2 Hours at 7°C | | | | | | |
|---|---|---|---|---|---|---|---|---|
| | | % NaOH | | | | | | |
| | | 0 | 2 | 4 | 6 | 8 | 10 | 12 |
| | | | | | D.P. Values | | | |
| Acetate grade cotton linters IV | Cuoxam viscosity | 235 | 238 | 231 | 224 | 224 | 158 | 100 |
| | Electron microscope | 292 | 215 | 200 | 173 | 150 | 122 | 108 |
| Acetate grade sulfite wood pulp V | Cuoxam viscosity | 217 | 205 | 192 | 172 | 128 | 110 | 100 |
| | Electron microscope | 185 | 165 | 138 | 108 | 73 | 67 | 41 |
| Sulfite grade tire yarn wood pulp VI | Cuoxam viscosity | 220 | 197 | 184 | 190 | 144 | 90 | 85 |
| | Electron microscope | 201 | 182 | 158 | 153 | 151 | 74 | 61 |
| Sulfate grade tire yarn wood pulp VII | Cuoxam viscosity | 180 | 173 | 177 | 182 | 140 | 109 | 83 |
| | Electron microscope | 193 | 156 | 167 | 143 | 152 | 79 | 66 |
| Sulfite grade textile yarn wood pulp VIII | Cuoxam viscosity | 255 | 244 | 221 | 189 | 125 | 84 | 84 |
| | Electron microscope | 171 | 178 | 153 | 160 | 105 | 69 | 48 |

* Industrial and Engineering Chemistry, Vol. 48, page 333, February 1956.
O. A. Battista, Sydney Coppick, J. A. Howsmon, F. F. Morehead, and Wayne A. Sisson. Copyrighted by American Chemical Society. Reprinted with permission.

this distribution, as does their solubility behavior, especially in concentrated solutions. A complete description of a high polymer requires, therefore, a knowledge not only of the average molecular weight, but also of the *distribution* of the individual molecular weights about this average.

There are three major ways of separating high polymers into their respective polymolecular components, by precipitation, fractional solution, and temperature differential methods.

## Precipitation Methods

**Stepwise Precipitation Method.** By far the most widely used method for the measurement of the polymolecularity or chain length distribution of a high polymer is the *stepwise precipitation method*. With precipitation procedures, the high polymer is brought into solution, usually at a concentration of 0.5 per cent or less. Precipitation of the polymer molecules from solution is then carried out by the slow addition of a precipitant until an initial turbidity is reached at a controlled temperature.

The solubility of chain polymers in suitable solvents or solvent mixtures falls off with increasing molecular weight or chain length. If a precipitant is run from a burette into a solution of a chain polymer, the longer the chain length of the polymer, the smaller volume of precipitant necessary to cause opalescence.

The choice of a precipitant for the fractionation of a high polymer on a chain length or molecular weight basis is of great importance. Table 8 illustrates the role of precipitants in insolubilizing long-chain molecules on the basis of per cent by weight and/or chain length (molecular weight), using the precipitation of cellulose from cuprammonium hydroxide solvent as an example.

Although not a conventional practice, it is recommended that the mixture be warmed slightly after the initial turbidity is observed to encourage the attainment of true equilibrium conditions, and then cooled slowly to the original precipitation temperature. The precipitate is then recovered, sometimes after centrifuging to effect a cleaner separation, and the average molecular weight as well as the weight per cent is determined for the fraction.

Having separated the first fraction from the polymer molecules

TABLE 8. FRACTIONATION OF CELLULOSE USING CUOXAM SOLVENT EXPERIMENTAL RAYON TIRE YARN; 100% WOOD PULP BASE; AVERAGE BASIC D.P. = 490

| Frac-tion | Sodium Potassium Tartrate Soln. | | Acetone | | n-Propyl Alcohol | |
|---|---|---|---|---|---|---|
| | % Recov. | Basic D.P. | % Recov. | Basic D.P. | % Recov. | Basic D.P. |
| 1 | 19.7 | 480 | 46.6 | 535 | 18.8 | 615 |
| 2 | 19.3 | 478 | 13.2 | 392 | 20.2 | 465 |
| 3 | 18.3 | 473 | 8.5 | 314 | 20.8 | 316 |
| 4 | 17.5 | 470 | 18.4 | 250 | 16.6 | 272 |
| 5 | 13.4 | 470 | 8.1 | 142 | 9.7 | 247 |
| 6 | 13.7 | 478 | --- | --- | 6.1 | 132 |

*Journal of the American Chemical Society*, **68**, 915 (1946).

still remaining in solution, a further increment of precipitant is now added as before to the remaining solution, and the process repeated to obtain the second fraction, and so forth, for as many fractions as are desired or required.

A plot of the weight per cent of each fraction recovered *vs.* the corresponding molecular weight parameter (i.e., relative viscosities expressed in basic D.P. units) of each fraction gives a typical step-wise integral distribution curve as shown in Figure 20. Differentiation of this curve gives the differential weight average form shown in Figure 20, which is the easiest way to interpret chain length distribution data visually. Literature reviews are available on molecular weight distribution measurements for cellulose* and on the fractionation of high polymers.†

**Summative Fractionation Method.** This method was first introduced by Coppick, Battista, and Lytton in a paper presented before the Division of Cellulose Chemistry, American Chemical Society, at the 106th ACS meeting in Pittsburgh in 1943 (published 1950); subsequently, other authors explored this simplified fractionation technique.‡

---

*(Symposium), *Ind. Eng. Chem.*, **45**, 2482–2537, (Nov. 1953).

†Cragg, L. H., and Hammerschag, H., *Chem. Revs.*, **39**, 79–135, (1946).

‡Coppick, S., Battista, O. A., and Lytton, M. R., *Ind. Eng. Chem.*, **42**, 2533–2535 (1950); Billmeyer, F. W., Jr. and Stockmayer, W. H., *J. Polymer Sci.*, **5**, 121–137 (1950); Spencer, R. S., *J. Polymer Sci.*, **3**, 606 (1948); Tasman, J. E., and Corey, A. J., *Pulp & Paper Mag. Can.,.*48, No. 3, 166–170 (1947); Rånby, B. G., Woltersdorf, O. W., and Battista, O. A., *Svensk Papperstidn.*, **60**, 373–378, (May 31, 1957).

With the summative fractionation method, the polymer is dissolved and a relatively large volume (one third) of weak precipitant is added in order that a small portion of the polymer will precipitate. The mixture is centrifuged and the precipitate is discarded. The polymer is quantitatively regenerated from an aliquot of the clear supernatant liquor. From the weight of the polymer

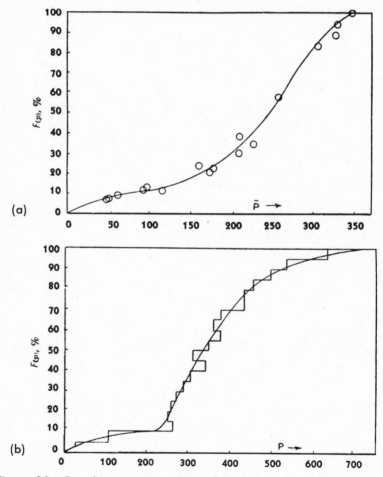

Figure 20. Graphic representations of chain-length distribution data for typical rayon prepared from wood pulp.
　　(a) Summative distribution plot.
　　(b) Integral distribution plot.

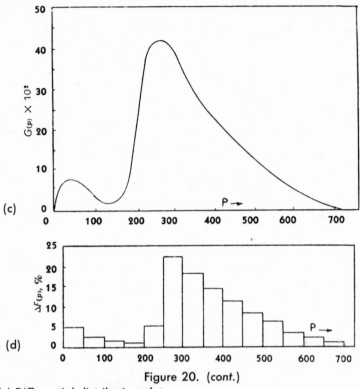

Figure 20. (cont.)

(c) Differential distribution plot.

(d) Pictorial or bar graph representation of chain length distribution data.

obtained the weight per cent in solution is calculated. This value is represented as $F_{(p)}$. A degree of polymerization measurement on this fraction is represented as $\overline{P}$, the weight average or viscosity value.

The procedure is repeated with a fresh sample of polymer, but this time a stronger precipitant is used in order to precipitate more polymer. Thus, by varying the composition of the precipitant, any number of values of $F_{(p)}$ with its companion $\overline{P}$ are obtained. The plot of $F_{(p)}$ against $\overline{P}$ gives the summative distribution curve (see Figure 20, (pp. 92–3)). To facilitate handling and to simplify calculations, the summative fractionations should be carried out at constant volume.

The summative method has unusual merit in that the conditions existing at any one cut are predetermined by the nature of the sample and not by the conditions existing after other fractions have been removed. This is of considerable importance in the reproducibility of experiments. In the conventional stepwise precipitation procedure, conditions of partial precipitation exist. Thus, material above a certain molecular weight may be almost totally precipitated whereas the components below this molecular weight are distributed between the two phases. No matter what the molecular weight of a particular species is, it will be more concentrated in the precipitate than in the supernatant liquid. Furthermore, the distribution coefficient will favor the precipitated phase to a greater extent as the molecular weight rises, and/or the amount of material precipitated increases. The amount of material precipitated up to a given point in a regular stepwise fractionation will, therefore, be a complicated function of the number and weight of the various fractions that have been obtained.

The resolving power of the summative process may not be as good as that of a stepwise fractionation because the low molecular weight components may be occluded with the precipitate. Nevertheless, fractional solution of the highly soluble short-chain components from the precipitant into the supernatant liquor will occur as conditions of equilibrium are approached during centrifuging. Also, divergences between stepwise solution and stepwise precipitation procedures are not serious in the range of low molecular weights, but become extremely serious in the range of high molecular weights.

## Fractional Solution Methods

An increasing amount of data in the literature has indicated that extraction procedures of the fractional solution methods are not efficient for separating the long molecules from the short. Consequently, the usefulness of this method has become largely limited to *relative* comparisons of samples.

With this method, the polymer is prepared when possible in

finely divided form or as a thin film. A solvent or series of solvents capable of swelling the polymer are used for the extraction treatments, in such a sequence that the shortest molecules are extracted first. It is customary to change the solvent power of the extraction solvent by changing composition, but a temperature differential is also sometimes utilized to remove succeeding fractions.

The handling of data by the solution fractionation method follows that used for the stepwise precipitation procedure. The cumulative or integral weight per cents, made up of the combined weight of all fractions up to and including the original average molecular weight $M_w$, are plotted against the corresponding specific molecular weights of the fractions to give a typical integral distribution curve. As before, differentiation of this cumulative integral curve gives the differential distribution plot.

A problem associated with all graphic conversion of smooth-curve data is, of course, that any scatter among points on which the smooth integral curve is based becomes accentuated in the graphic conversion to a differential plot. This is one of the reasons why care is necessary in the interpretation of the significance of so-called maxima that sometimes show up in differential distribution curve plots.

An ingenious fractionation method involving a solution mechanism has been advanced by C. A. Baker and R. J. P. Williams [*J. Chem. Soc.*, London, 2352–2362, (Aug. 1956)]. It uses a combination of column chromatography and a temperature differential to establish an equilibrium between a moving solution of the polymer and a stationary precipitated phase along the length of the column. A temperature differential between the top and bottom of the column is used to magnify the resolving power of the column.

The Baker and Williams method has been applied successfully to polystyrenes, and no doubt its applicability to other systems will be reported in the future. It proffers the advantages of fractionating continuously, by a system which conceivably could become automatic. Theoretically, it also permits a limitless number of fractions to be obtained. However, experimental difficulties have discouraged some workers from using this fractionation procedure.

## Temperature Differential Methods

The solubility of a high polymer in solution is temperature-dependent. As the temperature is lowered, for example, the thermodynamic properties of the solvent change, making it a poorer solvent. Eventually, a temperature will be reached at which precipitation of the least soluble components will occur because then the solvent and the polymer are no longer miscible in all proportions.

A stepwise precipitation and recovery of respectively precipitated fractions may then be performed, and the data handled exactly as with the stepwise precipitation technique.

Photometric methods for characterizing polymolecularity by measuring the turbidity of solutions with progressive reduction in solvent power has been used as a rapid screening method for characterizing chain length distribution. Such procedures have many disadvantages, however, and in each instance must be checked against another independent or "referee" method.

# 5. The Solid State of High Polymers

## ORIENTATION OF MOLECULES AND MICELLES

When polymer molecules are crystallized or coagulated from solution in the absence of exterior directional forces, the nuclei that are initiated grow into crystals that form in a random fashion. In other words, the chains in the crystallites do not lie largely along any particular plane. However, if during the crystallization step (as in the formation of a fiber or film) the polymer mass as a gel or as a melt is subjected to a stress, the molecules as well as the crystallites line up or become oriented in the general direction of the applied stress, as illustrated in Figure 21.

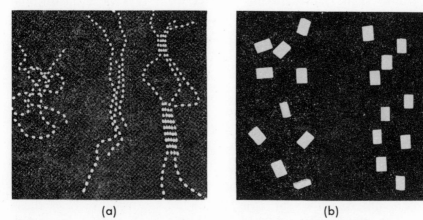

(a)                                             (b)

Figure 21. Schematic representation of orientation of molecules and crystallites:

      (a) Unoriented, oriented, and partially crystallized chains.

      (b) Unoriented and oriented crystallites.

In the case of fibers and films, at least, the extent to which the molecules and crystallites are oriented in a given longitudinal plane has a very important bearing on the properties of the product. For this reason, the measurement of orientation of crystallites in high polymers is extremely important: an increase in orientation of crystallites may greatly improve tensile strength, modulus or stiffness, etc.

Sometimes the measurement of birefringence (two refractive indices in a cross section of a product giving rise to double refraction) can be used as a quick gauge of orientation of crystallites. The most widely used technique, and in most instances the most reliable qualitative consideration, is x-ray diffraction.

Study of the birefringence of microscopically visible objects can give information about the orientation of the molecules if enough is known of the chemical composition. X-ray analysis is limited to the study of regions in which a crystalline lattice is well established; for the investigation of highly crystalline micellar structures this method is believed to be superior to all others.

In other words, x-rays do not tell us anything about the orientation or organization of chains in the *non-crystalline* part of the fiber because such chains do not diffract the x-rays in a measurable manner. They *do* tell reliably how well the individual crystallites are lined up in a given direction—their average orientation. Illustrations of typical x-ray diffraction diagrams showing the crystallites in a cellulose fiber and cellulose derivative in varying degrees of orientation are shown in Figures 22 and 23.

In macromolecular compounds like cellulose or polyethylene, crystallites may be as large as 100–500 A. In polyvinyl chloride, a macromolecule that can be crystallized only with difficulty, the crystallites may be as small as 20–50 A. Nylon and "Dacron" usually contain crystals of intermediate size ranging from 40–150 A.

The interpretation of x-ray diffraction patterns such as those shown in Figures 22 and 23 presents difficulties, and requires familiarity with the technique, as the broadening of the x-ray pattern can be caused not only by the size of the crystallites that may diffract the x-ray beam, but also by the thermal motion of the macromolecules and by crystal imperfections.

In Figure 22, for example, the significant observation is the progressive disappearance of the continuous inner ring (indicating random orientation of the crystallites followed by a diffuse scattering of the diffracted x-rays) in going from sample A to C. The appearance of the two inner "white spots" in sample C means that now—as a result of stretching—the tiny crystallites have been lined up

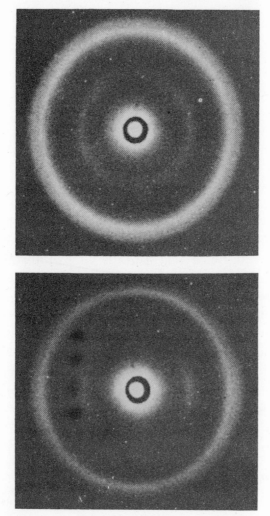

Figure 22. Typical x-ray diffraction diagrams showing viscose rayon fibers having crystallites at varying levels of orientation.
       A. Allowed to shrink freely.
       B. Not allowed to shrink in length.

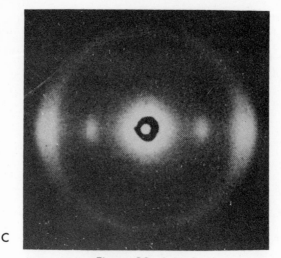

C

Figure 22. (cont.)
C. Stretched and dried under tension.

along the axis of stretching sufficiently well to permit the x-ray beam
to be diffracted in a directed manner. This process would corre-
spond to that illustrated schematically in part (b) of Figure 21.

The x-ray diagrams shown in Figure 22 are *fiber diagrams*,
produced by subjecting a small bundle of fibers to an x-ray beam.
Figure 23, on the other hand, is a *powder x-ray diagram;* the cellulose triacetate in powder form was subjected to the incident x-ray
beam. In a powder diagram, the orientation of the crystallites along
a unidirectional axis does not occur. Crystallinity and crystallization
are revealed in a powder x-ray diagram by the *sharpness* of the
concentric rings that appear. For example, the crystallinity of
sample B shown in Figure 23 is much less than that in sample C.

## A New Parameter for the Measurement of Crystallite Orientation

In the case of cellulose-based fibers like rayons, a new chemical
method of measuring crystallite orientation has been devised. It
consists of the chemical destruction of the accessible or amorphous
areas in the fiber by acid hydrolysis (see Figure 24, p. 105), as a
result of which the crystallites are left behind in the form of crys-

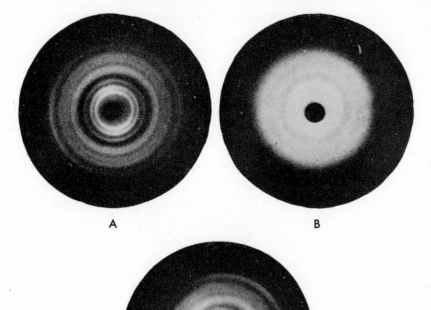

Figure 23. Typical x-ray diffraction diagrams showing the effect of heat treatments on the crystallization of cellulose triacetate molecules. [Baker, W. O., Fuller, C. S., and Pape, N. R., *J. Am. Chem. Soc.*, **64**, 776 (1942).]

    A. Solidified near melting point.
    B. Quenched at −75°C.
    C. (B), Annealed 2 hours at 225°C.

talline aggregates; the fibrous nature of the samples is completely destroyed by this procedure.

The porosity of the resulting hydrocellulose aggregates to water is then measured under standardized conditions. Invariably it has been found that when the crystallites are well-oriented within the fiber *prior* to hydrolysis, they give a hydrocellulose powder which swells only little in water, and water flows easily through pads of such aggregates. As a matter of fact, the hydrocellulose aggregates from a highly oriented fiber like "Fortisan" or a super tire cord are so well-defined that they resemble little glass prisms.

On the other hand, hydrocellulose powders prepared from poorly oriented fibers invariably swell in water to give a starch-like paste. Water passes only very slowly through pads prepared from such powders.

The hydrocellulose water flow number (HF No.) is defined simply as the time in seconds for 100 ml of water to flow through a hydrocellulose pad prepared and treated in a standardized manner; a high HF No. reflects poor crystallite orientation in the original product, and a low HF No., good crystallite orientation. This procedure is simple to run and can be handled by a technician. It has been calibrated against the x-ray diffraction referee method, as well as against a linear swelling procedure which also is a measure of crystallite orientation.*

This approach to the characterization of crystallite orientation is relatively new, and has not yet been applied to high polymer systems other than cellulose. Each polymer system will probably require a different procedure for substantially reducing the structure of the polymer to crystallites. In addition, the choice of liquid with which to measure the permeability of a "cake" of a particular species of crystallites will vary from product to product. The techniques, however, are very simple and it should be only a matter of time before they will be applied more generally.

## CRYSTALLITE SIZE

Crystals prepared from simple molecules, such as sugars and salts, have very definite dimensions, and are characterized by sharp boundaries. The crystallites in high polymers, on the other hand, are not so clean-cut. They do not have plain faces and sharp edges because they are transitional in nature. In other words, it is highly

---

* Battista, O. A., Howsmon, J.A., and Coppick, Sydney, *Ind. Eng. Chem.*, **45**, 2107-2112 (1953).

improbable that any high polymer can be 100 per cent crystalline or 100 per cent amorphous. A high polymer is currently pictured, then, as an aggregate of small crystalline regions embedded in a network structure of amorphous regions (see Figures 1, 12, 16, pp. 4, 61, 71).

Nevertheless, it is very important to be able to measure the "size" of the ordered areas, or crystallites, in high polymers. It now is recognized, for example, that the size, degree of compactness, and transitional geometry of crystallites in high polymers influence markedly such properties of a fiber or film as water absorption, dye-ability, swelling behavior, tensile strength, extensibility, and even fatigue behavior under conditions of repeated stress and re-laxation (e.g., a cord in an automobile tire). Two general approaches for establishing the size of crystallites in high polymers will be de-scribed in the following pages.

## Non-destructive Methods for Measuring Crystallite Size: X-ray Scattering

Long chain molecules, or segments of long chain molecules that bunch together into compact or ordered regions (see Figure 16, p. 71) give rise to crystallites having a high degree of internal geometric order. This geometric orientation explains why crystal-lites diffract x-rays and also why high polymers exhibit birefringence.

Today, x-ray techniques are usually considered among the most reliable for measuring crystallite size. Large crystals, for example, will diffract more, or interfere more with the uniformity of x-ray penetration than small crystals, and many attempts have been made to establish for polymers a calibration between *crystallite size* and *amount of x-ray diffraction*. The scattering of x-rays at small angles is a newer technique, still in the development stage, that has even better potential.

Crystallite sizes calculated from the broadening of x-ray diffrac-tion lines are minimum values because they reflect the size of the least disturbed regions within crystalline areas.

It is true that x-ray scattering at small angles is a *specific* method for measuring crystallite size, but it awaits further refinement, both in the simplification of manipulations and the clarification of theoretical interpretation, before it may be more widely and more reliably used.

The influence of the small size of crystallites on results obtained by means of x-ray diffraction techniques is worthy of special mention. MgO, for example, crystallizes well and gives extremely sharp crystallographic x-ray patterns. However, as the size of MgO crystals is reduced to about 1000 A the sharpness of the diffraction lines diminishes.

In high polymers, where the crystallite may be much smaller (see p. 98), this effect of crystallite size has already been superimposed on the observed x-ray patterns. If the size of high polymer crystallites was very small, they might therefore exhibit a diffuse, non-crystalline type of x-ray pattern—due only to crystallite size— even though the individual small crystallites were quite crystalline or perfect within themselves. It is because of such complicating factors that the analysis and interpretation of x-ray results of high polymer products require the assistance of a specialist in the field.

## Destructive Methods for Measuring Crystallite Size

In Figure 24 an attempt is made to illustrate in a simplified manner how a destructive method can be used to isolate and obtain at least a relative measure of the size of crystallites. In isolating the crystallites from a high polymer (as in the procedure for the measurement of crystallite orientation, p. 100), an attacking chemical penetrates disordered regions of the polymer easily, in such a manner that it destroys these areas at a much faster *rate* than it can destroy the ordered or crystalline regions.

The process whereby the disordered areas in a fiber like rayon are destroyed by hydrolysis is shown schematically in a stepwise manner in Figure 24. The acid (H⁺ ion) penetrates the disordered regions shown in *A*—the original structure. This causes the macromolecules in these areas to split into many small fragments, most of which are dissolved away. Some of the fragments crystallize into extremely small crystals as shown in *B*. In addition, the fringe-ends of the crystalline areas may recrystallize as illustrated in *C*.

In any case, the end result of the destructive treatment is the ex-

A. ORIGINAL STRUCTURE

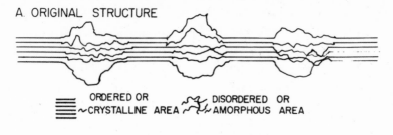

ORDERED OR ~CRYSTALLINE AREA      DISORDERED OR AMORPHOUS AREA

B. STRUCTURE AFTER MILD HYDROLYSIS OF DISORDERED AREA

RECRYSTALLIZED ~ MATERIAL

C. STRUCTURES AFTER DRASTIC HYDROLYSIS OR AT THE LEVEL-OFF D.P. ($\overline{D.P.}$)

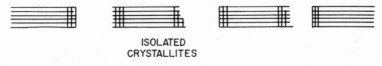

ISOLATED CRYSTALLITES

Figure 24. Schematic illustration of crystallite size and crystallite size measurement by destructive hydrolysis methods.

posure of crystallites in the same or a somewhat modified state in which they existed prior to chemical treatment. Naturally, the extent to which such recrystallization phenomena occur will reflect a proportionate error if the measured length of the crystallites is interpreted as being the length of the crystallites in the *original* polymer based, for example, on a non-destructive method of measurement, such as by x-rays.

To date, cellulose is the high polymer upon which a destructive technique has been most widely used. Fortunately, in the case of cellulose, hydrochloric acid is an almost ideal chemical for attacking, destroying, and then dissolving away the breakdown residues of the disordered regions. Hot HCl (2 to 4$N$) causes an extremely rapid scission of the 1:4 glycosidic bonds in the disordered or "accessible" regions. In addition it has essentially no swelling action on the crystallites at concentrations adequate for substantially destroying the amorphous regions.

This hydrolysis reaction, which is characteristic for each species of cellulose, is reflected by an almost immediate initial rapid drop in average degree of polymerization to what is called a *level-off* D.P. value, usually identified by the symbol $\overline{\text{D.P.}}$ The $\overline{\text{D.P.}}$ value of any polymer is defined simply as the relatively constant value reached for the D.P. after chemical attack designed to destroy the disordered areas while damaging or changing the ordered areas to the least possible extent. Drastic hydrolysis conditions give good results (i.e., $2.50N$ at $105°C$ for 15 minutes).

This method can prove useful in characterizing this important property of high polymers on a *relative* basis, at least. An illustration of how this technique has been applied to advantage in the case of cellulose fiber research studies is revealed by the data in Table 9. In the case of secondary cellulose acetates (54.5 per cent combined HOAc), where crystallites are not detectable by x-ray diffraction measurements, essentially no crystallites are found by the hydrolysis procedure.

The nexus of problems associated with the characterization of the properties of high polymers is a recurring limitation that makes *relative* data rather than *absolute* data the most convenient and most practical to get. Fortunately for high polymer technology, relative data frequently are entirely adequate.

Little or no work has been done with destructive methods for isolating crystallites in polymers other than cellulose, but this method should be effective provided the conditions used to destroy and remove the disordered areas leave the ordered areas or crystallites relatively unchanged.

## POLYPHASE STRUCTURE OF HIGH POLYMERS

### The Determination of Fine Structure

In order to obtain as complete a picture as possible of the whole structure of a high polymer, it is desirable to consider: (1) the spatial arrangement of the atoms within the molecules, keeping in

TABLE 9. LEVEL-OFF BASIC DEGREE OF POLYMERIZATION DATA FOR NATURAL AND REGENERATED CELLULOSE FIBERS (RELATIVE CRYSTALLITE LENGTHS)*

| Form of Cellulose | Original Basic D.P. Range | Average Basic $\overline{D}$.P. Range After 15 Mins. in 2.5N HCl @ 105°C | % Hydrocellulose Residue |
|---|---|---|---|
| **Natural Fibers** | | | |
| Ramie, Hemp | 3500 — 4500 | 350 — 300 | 90 — 96 |
| Cotton, Purified | 3000 — 4000 | 250 — 200 | 90 — 94 |
| Bleached Sulfite Pulps | 1000 — 1500 | 280 — 200 | 88 — 92 |
| Bleached Sulfate Wood Pulps | 700 — 900 | 190 — 140 | 88 — 90 |
| Mercerized Cellulose (18% NaOH at 20°C, 2 Hrs.) | 700 — 1000 | 90 — 70 | 88 — 92 |
| Vibratory-milled Wood Cellulose | 1200 — 1400 | 100 — 80 | 88 |
| **Regenerated Fibers** | | | |
| Fortisan, Fiber G | 500 — 600 | 60 — 40 | 88 — 90 |
| Textile Yarns | 450 — 550 | 50 — 30 | 81 — 83 |
| Tire Yarns | 500 — 600 | 30 — 15 | 78 — 81 |
| **Cellulose Acetates** | | | |
| Combined HOAc | | | |
| 62.0% | 300 — 375 | 200 — 300 | 85 — 90 |
| 54.5% | — | Not measurable | 0.1 — 0.3 |
| 29 % | — | 46 | 39 |
| 0.5% | — | 35 | 79 |

* *Ind. and Eng. Chem.*, **48**, 333, (Feb. 1956); See also *Ind. and Eng. Chem.*, **42**, 502–7, (March 1950).

mind the three-dimensional structure; (2) the arrangement of the molecules to form crystallites; and (3) the arrangement of the crystallites in the macroscopic solid body, as for example in fibrils, fibers, laminae, or films, or in commercial products.

Many chemical and physical methods are used to investigate the fine structure of fibers and films in an effort to reconstruct the internal geometry, or the ordered-disordered architecture, of useful high polymer products. As yet no ideal procedure is available, although new instrumental as well as radiochemical techniques show great promise. These procedures are designed primarily to characterize the following important elements within the constitution of a useful fiber or film:

(1) *Orientation*. The efficiency with which the most densely packed centers (crystalline areas) are lined up in the longitudinal direction of a fiber notably affects the tensile strength of fibers and films.

(2) *Ratio of Crystalline to Amorphous Material.*

(3) *Crystallite Size.*

(4) *Mass Order Distribution*. The polyphase nature or the order-disorder distribution of the molecules is an important property in terms of swelling, chemical reactivity, and extensibility.

The following methods for determination of the ratio of crystalline to amorphous material are worthy of note.

**Chemical Methods.** Chemical methods, such as hydrolysis, formylation, and oxidation, all rely on destroying or reacting with sensitive regions quickly, and then achieving a very slow reaction rate upon attacking the crystalline components. By estimating how much material is quickly destroyed, the crystalline remainder is calculated usually by difference and a figure for the ratio of crystalline to non-crystalline material is set. Such methods give relative values which are useful provided their interpretation is conditioned by the realization that they *are* relative values.

A wealth of literature exists on chemical methods that have been used for characterizing the polyphase structure of cellulose, in particular. It is beyond the scope of this volume to detail such methods here, but a complete bibliography of the literature about them appears at the end of this book (see in particular ref. 12).

**Physical Methods.** Of numerous attempts to apply physical methods, x-ray diffraction has been widely used and with considerable success. It works best, however, when the total crystallinity is high and the size of the crystals large ($>500$ A for example). This method loses sensitivity and reliability when (1) the proportion of the non-crystalline areas is high (x-rays are not able to characterize these areas); (2) the size of the crystallites is very small ($<100$ A, for example); or (3) the crystallites are studded with imperfections.

The basic concept of crystalline-disorganized structure can be simplified by defining the amount of non-crystalline material as being directly proportional to the accessibility and number of side groups that are not tied to other side groups having strong affinity and close stereophysical association with each other. Accordingly, the most promising absolute methods on the present-day horizon for characterizing the ratio of crystalline to non-crystalline material in high polymer systems would be: (1) the use of infrared techniques, (2) replacement of available hydrogen atoms by deuterium atoms, and (3) the use of radioactive tritium to replace available hydrogen atoms (in the non-crystalline regions of cellulose, for example).

It is unlikely that these methods will replace the simple relative procedures. But their great value will be in providing reliable "referee" methods whereby simpler procedures may be accurately calibrated so as to permit quantitative characterization of this very important internal or "physiological" make-up of fibers and films.

**Moisture Regain.** Another simple and very useful method for measuring the ratio of crystalline to non-crystalline areas is based on the absorption of water vapor or other small solvent molecules that are unaffected by orientation. In the case of cellulose, for example, the assumption is made that the hydroxyl groups along chains in the crystalline areas are firmly bonded to hydroxyl groups on neighboring chains. They are, therefore, quite unavailable (unless they are on the surface of the crystallites) to capture and hold on to water molecules, while those in the non-crystalline areas would be free to do so. Therefore, under standardized conditions a reasonably good proportionality between moisture regain and the amount of non-crystalline cellulose should be obtainable. This, in effect, is the case as the data in Table 10 show.

TABLE 10.  RELATION OF MOISTURE REGAIN AND CRYSTALLITE SIZE OF
VARIOUS FIBERS*

| Fiber | Moisture Regain % | Hydrolysis Rate Constant ($X\ 10^{-5}$) | Level-off Basic D.P. — Crystallite Size |
|---|---|---|---|
| Cotton | 6.7 | .54 | 250 |
| "Fortisan" | 9.0 | 1.1 | 110 |
| Textile Rayon | 12.0 | 1.9 | 90 |
| Tire Rayon | 13.0 | 3.6 | 55 |

## THE ORDER-DISORDER DISTRIBUTION CONCEPT
## FOR HIGH POLYMERS

The most acceptable current concept of the internal geometry of high polymers has emerged from the pioneering work of many persons in the fields of cellulose and cellulose derivatives. Attention is called particularly to the early contributions of the following authors in the bibliography: W. O. Baker, S. Coppick, P. H. Hermans, J. A. Howsmon, H. Mark, and W. A. Sisson, to mention only a few. Perhaps the most detailed presentation of this concept is that by Howsmon and Sisson.*

In essence, this concept postulates that there are no necessarily sharply defined transitions between crystalline and amorphous domains. It proposes a mass distribution of order varying from perfect crystallinity to complete disorganization. Schematically, this concept is shown in Figure 25, and a quantitative plot of such an order distribution can be expressed as a differential distribution curve as illustrated in Figure 26. In other words, each high polymer solid product has a characteristic mass-order differential dis-

---

* Howsmon, J. A. and Sisson, W. A. in Vol. V, Chapter IV, High Polymer Series, Ott, Spurlin, and Grafflin, Eds., New York, Interscience Publishers, Inc., 1954. Table reprinted with permission.

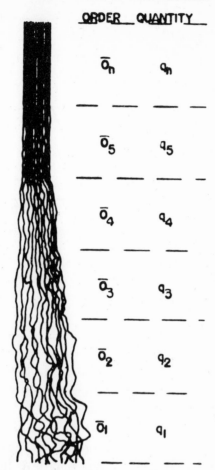

ORDER QUANTITY

$\overline{O}_n$  $q_n$

$\overline{O}_5$  $q_5$

$\overline{O}_4$  $q_4$

$\overline{O}_3$  $q_3$

$\overline{O}_2$  $q_2$

$\overline{O}_1$  $q_1$

Figure 25. Schematic mass order distribution diagram for cellulose according to Howsmon and Sisson.

tribution composition and its internal geometry can be expressed quantitatively only when it is known for the complete scale.

If we accept the lateral order distribution hypothesis described above, it would follow that a gradation in the swelling of the regions of varying degrees of order will occur when the entire structure is allowed to swell in media to which are progressively added solutions of more powerful swelling power (see **Swelling and Moisture Sensitivity,** p. 115). If the swelling power is strong

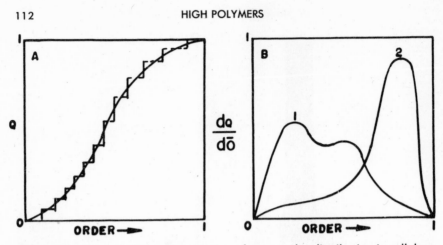

Figure 26. Quantitative representation of mass order distribution in cellulose according to Howsmon and Sisson:

    (A) Summative mass-order curve for lateral order.

    (B) Differential lateral order distribution curves for celluloses having (1) low and (2) high lateral order.

enough, even the most perfectly ordered area, or true crystallites, might become swollen. Should this occur, shorter crystallites would result upon subsequent drastic hydrolysis, because the hydrolyzing acid would be able to penetrate deeper into the crystalline regions which have been loosened by swelling.

Experiments with celluloses swollen in sodium hydroxide solutions have confirmed this expectation. Accordingly, the process of following the change in the average length of the crystallites in cellulose by measuring the resulting level-off D.P. has come into use as an alternative, and simple, means for the characterization of lateral order distribution.

Interestingly enough, data obtained by this procedure, such as are illustrated in Figure 27, agree as a first approximation, at least, with the mass order distributions for the same samples obtained by a more direct and independent method such as moisture regain, etc.

For example, the curves in Figure 27 are interpreted as meaning that the lateral order distribution of a sulfite wood pulp is less pronounced than the distribution of order of the macromolecular

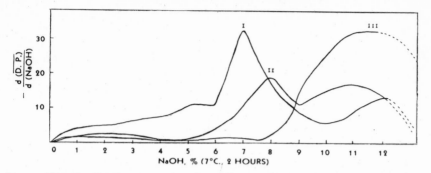

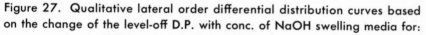

Figure 27. Qualitative lateral order differential distribution curves based on the change of the level-off D.P. with conc. of NaOH swelling media for:

I: Sulfite pulp—viscose grade.

II: Sulfate (prehydrolyzed) Kraft wood pulp.

III: Cotton linters pulp—Viscose grade.

[*Ind. and Eng. Chem.*, **48**, 333 (Feb. 1956).]

cellulose chains in a cotton fiber. On the other hand, the lateral order distribution of a prehydrolyzed sulfate wood pulp (prepared under conditions which would encourage recrystallization and an increase in lateral order) is shown to fall in an intermediate range. The higher the concentration (or swelling power) of sodium hydroxide solution needed to reduce the Level-off D.P. ($\overline{D.P.}$), the greater the lateral order distribution as pointed out in Figure 26 *B*.

The application of the mass order distribution concept to high polymer technology and the development of techniques to measure this distribution, both qualitatively and quantitatively, are relatively new. No doubt there will be intensified activity along these lines in the future.

# 6. Physical Properties of High Polymers

Four major physical properties are intimately tied to internal fiber structure. They are of such great practical importance that they deserve special attention.

## Tensile Strength and Extensibility

Using the cellulose molecule as an example, it is evident from Figures 6 and 7 (pp. 16, 17) that the molecule has numerous hydroxyl groups capable of strong interchain hydrogen-bonding. When fibers are constructed in such a way as to encourage a maximum of bonding between these groups, they invariably possess very high strengths, strengths that approach that of steel (e.g., "Fortisan," Fiber G, etc.). However, capitalizing on the strength-giving properties of interchain hydrogen-bonding in cellulose usually results in a severe sacrifice of rubberlike properties, because the ratio of crystalline to non-crystalline areas becomes substantially increased. As a result, extensibility is low, and bending and abrasion properties deteriorate for most textile fiber uses.

In the case of "Vinyon," on the other hand (see Figure 3, p. 8), bulky ester groups prevent good lateral packing and intimate exertion of lateral hydrogen-bonding forces. A weaker, more heat-sensitive (low softening point) fiber results.

## Plastic or Flow Behavior

The lateral hydrogen-bonding forces of the numerous hydroxyl groups in cellulose are so great that fibers and films made from cellulose are not heat-sensitive or thermoplastic; they decompose by pyrolysis before melting can occur. Silk (Figure 8, p. 31) also is loaded with strong lateral hydrogen-bonding groups, and it also

114

is not thermoplastic. But "Vinyon" (Figure 3, p. 8) and commercial cellulose acetate fibers (in which the degree of substitution is about 2.5) are relatively heat-sensitive or thermoplastic because their internal geometry makes it impossible for hydrogen-bonding to hold the chains in a locked arrangement.

Nylon and "Dacron," on the other hand, lie between cellulose and "Vinyon" as regards heat sensitivity. To be sure, nylon possesses strong hydrogen-bonding side groups, but at regular intervals between these groups (C=O, NH) there are long segments of heat-sensitive hydrocarbon (polyethylene) chains. In this respect, polyamides in general reflect a cross-breed between cellulose and polyethylene, and their resulting properties reflect the extent and nature of this mixture.

## Swelling and Moisture Sensitivity

If cellulose molecules were aggregated together so that all hydroxyl groups were interlocked to form, essentially, a 100 per cent crystalline material, it would be almost as water-insensitive as glass. Fortunately, many of these groups in cellulose fibers are too far from each other in disorganized regions to exert their hydrogen bonding capabilities. Such free hydroxyl groups attract water (H—OH) molecules and hold onto them tenaciously. This is why cellulose fibers will absorb moisture, and the extent to which they will absorb moisture is proportional to the number of groups *free* to do so (i.e., proportional to the crystalline/non-crystalline ratio, on the premise that hydroxyl groups within the crystalline regions are linked to adjacent hydroxyl groups).

Water, therefore, causes swelling and stretching of cellulose fibers by latching onto available hydroxyl groups in the non-crystalline regions of the fibers. Cotton has a lower water pick-up or sensitivity than ordinary rayons because it has fewer unattached hydroxyl groups and a different fine structure. However, when rayons are produced in such a way as to increase their crystallinity to approach that of cotton, their moisture sensitivity approaches that of cotton. "Vinyon," on the other hand, possessing very little crystallinity, is even more insensitive to water than crystalline cellulose because it has *hydrophobic* or water-indifferent groups along its chains, groups that are unattracted by the hydroxyl ions of the water molecule.

## Compatability with Dyestuffs

Whether or not a fiber or film can be dyed depends upon the extent to which bulky dye particles migrate into, and become lodged in, openings made in the internal structure. In addition, dye molecules that may be sufficiently small to penetrate into a fiber must also have an attraction or compatability with the functional groups along the polymer chain. In this latter respect, the absorption of dyes, the tenaciousness with which a fiber will capture and hold onto them, is analogous to the affinity of free hydroxyl groups in cellulose for water.

Swelling becomes the underlying mechanism for the penetration of dyes into a fiber; chemical compatability of the exposed sidegroups in dye molecules with the side groups in high polymer molecules controls the permanence of a dye in a fiber. Success in dyeing synthetic fibers such as "Dacron," "Acrilan," "Vinyon," and nylon is dependent largely on the use of swelling media to permit dye molecules to penetrate into their internal fiber structures. Summarizing, we can say that the physical and mechanical properties of high polymers will depend largely upon:

1. the average length of the long-chain molecules and the distribution of their size about the average length;
2. the fraction (or amount) of the polymer which is in a state of maximum organization (crystalline) compared to the fraction (or amount) that is relatively disorganized (non-crystalline); and
3. the extent of the *orientation* or lining up of the ordered areas and primary molecules.

The interdependent role of interchain forces, or in essence, the physical compatability of the chains in a lateral dimension, will also play a basic role in determining the ultimate physical properties of high polymers. For example, normal polyethylene represents one extreme of a high polymer in which the lateral attractive forces are of a non-polar nature and exhibit a minimum of effectiveness; it is soft and has a low melting point. On the other hand, polyvinylidene chloride and polyacrylonitrile possess extremely strong polar lateral forces of attraction; these polymers are strong, tough and brittle. An intermediate illustration would be nylon, which is in essence a block copolymer consisting of a segment of the chain which is paraffin in nature (non-polar) and another segment in which strong polar groups are present.

It now is generally recognized that before a high polymer can be useful, it must possess several suitable physical properties:

1. It must have a reasonably high softening point.
2. It must maintain its tensile strength over a wide range of temperature.
3. It must be readily soluble, in some cases at least, in economical solvents.
4. It must resist weathering and decomposition by exposure to sunlight.


## PHYSICAL TESTS FOR HIGH POLYMERS

Numerous tests are used for characterizing the physical properties of high polymers. A single manual or textbook devoted to the specific procedures or methods of testing high polymers is not available to the writer's knowledge. Such a book could rightfully comprise a separate volume. Accordingly, no attempt is made here to provide a complete and detailed listing of the procedures for measuring the physical and mechanical properties of high polymers. Rather, the objects of this part of the book are to describe the purpose of some of these tests, and to mention information of practical value that may be obtained from them.

### Methods of Testing

A standing problem in connection with the measurement of the physical properties of high polymers is the development of laboratory tests which will reflect as closely as possible the actual service condition or conditions under which the high polymer will be used. In the case of most mechanical tests, for example, it is highly desirable that the stress or strain applied to the high polymer during the test be held constant. High polymers as a rule possess a series of retarded elastic mechanisms in response to stress, as well as a more or less instantaneous elasticity and flow property. It is important, therefore, that reproducible and controllable physical states are maintained *during* the process of measuring the physical and mechanical properties of polymers. For example, in the case of tensile strength measurement of a high polymer, the rate of loading, the length of the test piece, and the relative humidity under which the test is performed, can influence greatly the level of the property being measured.

**Cross-Section of Fibers.** Microscopic examination of thin cross-sections prepared with a microtome provides a method of determining size and other cross-sectional characteristics of fibers.

**Electron Microscopy.** Great progress has been achieved in measuring the physical properties of high polymers in recent years through the application of the electron microscope. Thin cross-sections are prepared, utilizing the standard microscopic techniques. Such sections may subsequently have atoms of palladium deposited on them so that an electron microscope replica of the palladium shell can be made. Much valuable information about the submicroscopic structure of high polymers has been obtained by this means, and these findings have on many occasions been found to correlate with the physical properties of the polymer.

## Measurable Properties of High Polymers

**Anisotropic Properties.** *Anisotropy* is a characteristic that results when solvent molecules penetrate between chain molecules and push them apart laterally. Under such conditions there is a larger change in the diameter or cross section than in length. Measurements of this ratio can be sometimes interpreted in terms of the physical properties that can be expected from the high polymer.

**Creep, and Creep Recovery.** As has been mentioned, the extensibility of high polymers is a function of time at constant load, and generally the extension decreases as time goes on, but it never actually falls to zero. The fact that it never does fall to zero is what gives rise to the phenomenon of *creep*. On the other hand, when a high polymer has been stretched and released, it exhibits the phenomenon of *creep recovery*. Sometimes the creep recovery might be sufficient, as is frequently the case with rubber, to cause the high polymer to regain its original length. Usually, however, a high polymer does not return all the way to its original dimension after stretching. This is particularly true, for example, in the case of cellulosic fibers, which show very poor creep recovery. Like the property of creep itself, creep recovery is extremely dependent upon the environment of the high polymer.

**Denier.** In the textile industry, *denier* is defined simply as the weight in grams of 9000 meters of the fiber. The denier also may be used to correlate density and tensile strength because it is proportional to the density of a fiber and its cross-sectional area. (See **tensile strength in grams/denier,** p. 121.)

**Density.** By classic definition, *density* $=$ mass/volume. A valuable technique for measuring the density of high polymeric materials is to use a density gradient column. In this procedure a liquid column having materials varying in density throughout the height of the column is used. A sample of the high polymer is then equilibrated in this density gradient column, and by measuring the point in the column at which the high polymer neither sinks nor rises, the density of the liquid in the column at this point can be taken as a measure of the density of the high polymer.

**Dichroism.** *Dichroism* is a property of a high polymer that is evidenced as a result of the absorption of polarized light; it depends upon the vibration direction of the light. This *dichroic* effect shows up, for example, after the polymer has been dyed. In such instances the dye molecules become oriented, and the effect is most pronounced when the molecules in the polymer are highly oriented.

**Extensibility.** When a high polymer is stretched it exhibits *extensibility* up to a point beyond which further stretching will cause it to break. For example, in the case of rubber, its high elasticity or extensibility is due to the fact that the irregularly curled molecules are straightened out on stretching by applied force. When the force is released, the irregular configuration of the molecules becomes more or less restored as a result of spontaneous thermal movements.

When a high polymer is stretched under a constant load, the amount of extensibility observed will be a function of time, and if a high polymer is held at a fixed extensibility it will actually exhibit the phenomenon of *relaxation* as evidenced by a progressive loss in tensile strength.

**Fiber Length.** This is a relatively easy property to measure. It is usually done visually by lining up a fiber of reasonable length against some measuring yardstick, or it may be done in the case of small fibers using a microscope with a calibrated scale.

**Frictional and Static Electricity Properties.** Both of these properties of high polymers are almost impossible to characterize quantitatively because of their complexity. There are tests available for specific compounds that are of practical use, but such tests are not available for general use. Both of these properties of high polymers involve a comprehensive series of phenomena which we do not yet properly understand. Yet, both friction and static properties are of extreme importance for the practical utility of high polymers in numerous uses, e.g., in the carding and weaving of fibers into fabrics in the textile industry.

**Refractive Index.** It is customary to measure the refractive index of a high polymer by matching it against the refractive index of an immersion liquid. The usual procedure is to prepare a series of suitable liquids of known refractive index and mount a thin section of the high polymer for microscopic examination in the liquids. When the refractive index of the high polymer and the liquid appear to be identical (the high polymer powder, or cross-section of a fiber, becomes practically invisible), the refractive index can be determined from that of the known immersion medium.

**Tensile Strength.** *Tensile strength* is one of the most important physical properties of all high polymers. This property is usually most closely tied in with the total amount of crystalline material and the orientation of the crystalline material in a preferred direction. The tensile strength of materials, of course, is normally expressed in terms of psi. However, in the field of high polymer fiber chemistry it is more conventional to express the tensile strength in terms of density, where density means the strength per unit *size number*, where the size number is expressed as a weight per unit length.

It is customary to measure simultaneously the tensile strength and the extensibility of a high polymer, in fiber form, for example. To do this, a so-called stress-strain curve is measured; a typical example of such a curve is illustrated in Figure 28. Two general types of stress-strain curves are obtained for high polymers. In one type, a very sharp decrease in the modulus at low stress is promptly followed by an extended period of elongation at almost constant stress (e.g., unvulcanized rubber). The other type involves an almost constant high modulus to the break point (e.g., glass fiber). Of course, all manner of variations between these two extremes are possible.

**Tensile Strength in Grams/Denier.** Tensile strength (psi) = tenacity (grams per denier) × density × 12,791.

**Vapor Regain.** If a high polymer is maintained in an atmosphere of constant solvent composition (for example, constant relative humidity), after the lapse of an extended period of time an equilibrium of solvent to solute content (regain) will be reached, depending on the concentration of the solvent. The amount of solvent that can be taken up at equilibrium should be related to the fine structure of the high polymer. In fact, the moisture regain of cellulosic fibers is now used to elucidate certain fine structure characteristics of cellulose.

**Volume of Fibers.** There is, of course, bound to be a correlation between the volume and the density of fibers, and it is customary to make use of immersion media to obtain data on such properties. It is important, however, in measuring the volume of a fiber by immersion in a liquid, to choose a liquid which does not swell the fiber. Even when non-swelling liquids are used, there may still be

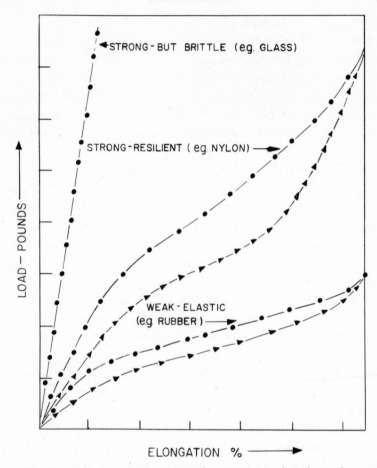

Figure 28. Typical stress-strain curves characterizing the physical properties of high polymeric materials.

some error because they may not penetrate quantitatively into the crevices of the fiber, thereby introducing an error in the measured volume. For this reason it is important to specify or define in each case exactly what is meant by the density or the volume of a high polymer.

In recent years there has been considerable interest in the utilization of an inert gas such as helium for measuring the density of polymers. Helium is capable of atomic penetration into the polymer structure, and therefore should provide an absolute value for the density.

**Young's Modulus.** This is a very important property of high polymers, and is related to the *stiffness of the molecular state of aggregation*. It is determined usually by the resistance to deformation under stress. The modulus is closely related to the nature of the polar forces or bonds in or between the long-chain molecules.

# 7. The Future of High Polymers

The future of high polymers appears to be brighter than ever because, in most areas, we still are off by a factor of 10 from achieving maximum theoretical strengths largely because it has been impossible to achieve perfect structures.

However, limiting ourselves to linear hydrocarbon polymers, we can speculate that if properly oriented they ought to be very strong, because of the great strength of the —C—C— linkage, which is calculated to be about $5.6 \times 10^{-4}$ dyne. Since the cross-sectional area of paraffin chains is roughly 20 sq A, each mm normal to the axis of orientation should contain about $5 \times 10^{12}$ chains, which would give a tensile strength of $2.8 \times 10^3$ kg/mm$^2$, or four million psi. Now actual measurements on all manner of materials seldom approach this figure within a factor of 10. For example, the best grade of steel wire has a strength of about 400,000 psi, while cellulose rarely exceeds 150,000 psi or rubber 50,000 psi. In the case of very fine-spun quartz fibers, the strength may approach the above theoretical figure for a hydrocarbon. The foregoing facts indicate that a frontier exists for making even greater strides by appropriate improvements in the variation of the mutual molecular attraction of long-chain molecules and also by improvements in their architecture as well as internal fine structures.

The use of natural and synthetic polymers in the fields of plastics, fibers, rubbers or elastomers, coatings, and lacquers, is bound to increase at a fast rate during the next generation. This is inevitable because we have reached a technological plateau from which we can predict the structure and the resulting properties of new high polymer products yet to be created; and even beyond this remarkable promise lies that of exploring the phenomena whereby such high polymers as cellulose, starch, and the proteins give rise to living cells, the basic substances which carry on the processes whereby life itself is initiated and maintained.

No one high polymer, of course, can satisfy *all* the requirements of an end-product—whether it be for the nose of a guided missile, a fabric for a tent, or an article of lingerie. This is no longer a serious limitation, however, for man now knows how to fashion from simple chemical raw materials polymer products to meet desired property specifications. One of the most significant advances in recent years that will make this versatility of product-creation felt more than ever, is the new technology of polymer specificities as reflected in the isotactic polymer products. These products are produced with the aid of policeman-like catalysts which direct the growth of polymers from their surfaces. Just as nature uses still-unsolved techniques to produce physiological specificity in protein tissues, so also we can expect polymer scientists to start with simple molecules and build them into products that will fill definite and specific needs.

The future of high polymers does, indeed, look more inviting today than it did at any time during the relatively short period during which man has attempted to master this new science. There is promise of pleasure, profit, and progress awaiting all who wish to delve into this limitless frontier of unsolved phenomena. Endless prospects of valuable new products await the studious and determined high polymer scientists of tomorrow, and it is safe to say the synthetic polymers of the next 25 years will be of even greater importance than those of the past.

# Bibliography

Literally hundreds of workers have made active and significant contributions to the science of high polymers over the past three or four decades. Inasmuch as this textbook is intended to be a formal introduction to the science and technology of high polymers, it was felt that the inclusion of thousands of literature references with the running text would detract from, rather than assist, those who are trying to grasp the fundamentals of these subjects for the first time.

For this reason, we are providing the following bibliography which provides what we believe are references to the most important contributions in the field. They are organized along topical lines that parallel closely the subject matter of the text proper. Essentially all of these references were studied by the author in the course of writing this text. Without the immense wealth of knowledge contributed by the authors in this bibliography, this textbook could not have been written, and it is a genuine pleasure to acknowledge, in essence, "co-authorship" with the contributors whose textbooks and publications are compiled in this bibliography.

In addition, the author acknowledges the impracticality and near-impossibility of paying due credit in this bibliography to all individuals who have added significant information to the fund of high polymer knowledge.

### Adhesives

1. Braude, F., *Adhesives*, Chemical Pub. Co., New York City (1943)

### Biochemistry

2. Norman, A. G., *Biochemistry of Cellulose*, Clarendon Press (1937)

### Cellulose

3. Brown, H. B., *Cotton*, McGraw-Hill Book Co., New York City (1938)

4. Hagglund, E., *Chemistry of Wood*, Academic Press, New York City (1951)
5. Hess, K., *Die Chemie der Zellulose*, Akadem. Verlagsgesellschaft, Leipzig (1928)
6. Heuser, E., *The Chemistry of Cellulose*, John Wiley and Sons, New York City (1944)
7. Jørgensen, L., *Studies on the Partial Hydrolysis of Cellulose*, Emil Moestue, Oslo (1950)
8. Karrer, P., *Polymere Kohlenhydrate*, Akadem. Verlagsgesellschaft, Leipzig (1925)
9. Marsh, J. T. and Wood, F. C., *An Introduction to the Chemistry of Cellulose*, D. Van Nostrand Co., New York City (1939); Chapman and Hall, London (1938)
10. Meyer, K. H. and Mark, H., *Der Aufbau de hochpolymeren organischen Naturstoffe*, Akadem. Verlagsgesellschaft, Leipzig (1930)
11. Miles, F. D., *Cellulose Nitrate*, Interscience Publishers, New York City (1955)
12. Ott, E., Spurlin, H. M., and Grafflin, M. W., Eds., *Cellulose and Its Derivatives*, Parts I, II, III, Interscience Publishers, New York City (1955 and 1954)
13. Siu, H., *Microbial Decomposition of Cellulose*, Reinhold Pub. Corp., New York City (1951)
14. Stannett, V., *Cellulose Acetate Plastics*, Temple Press, Ltd., London, England (1950)
15. Wise, L. E. and Jahn, E. C., *Wood Chemistry*, 2nd Ed. in 2 Vols., Reinhold Pub. Corp., New York City (1952)

## Chemistry

16. Bawn, C. E. H., *The Chemistry of High Polymers*, Interscience Publishers, New York City (1948)
17. Billmeyer, F. W., Jr., *Textbook of Polymer Chemistry*, Interscience Publishers, New York City (1957)
18. Burk, R. E. and Grummitt, O., Eds., *The Chemistry of Large Molecules* (1st Ed.), Interscience Publishers, New York City (1943)
19. Burk, R. E. and Grummitt, O., Eds., *Chemical Architecture* (Frontiers in Chemistry, Vol. V), Interscience Publishers, New York City (1948)
20. Burk, R. E. and Grummitt, O., Eds., *High Molecular Weight Organic Compounds* (Frontiers in Chemistry, Vol. VI), Interscience Publishers, New York City (1949)
21. Flory, P. J., *Principles of Polymer Chemistry*, Cornell Univ. Press., Ithaca, N. Y. (1953)

22. Fuoss, R. M. and Baitsell, G. A., Eds., *The Physical Chemistry of Polymers*, Yale University Press, New Haven, Conn. (1951)

23. Mark, H. and Whitby, G. S., *The Collected Papers of W. H. Carothers on High Polymeric Substances*, Interscience Publishers, New York City (1940)

24. Mark, H. and Tobolsky, A. V., *Physical Chemistry of High Polymeric Systems* (2nd Ed.), Interscience Publishers, New York City (1950)

25. Milone, M., et al, *International Symposium on Macromolecular Chemistry*, Consiglio Nazionale delle Ricerche, Rome, Italy (1955)

26. Wagner, R. H. and Weissberger, A., Eds., *Physical Methods of Organic Chemistry*, Interscience Publishers, New York City (1949)

## Copolymerization

27. Alfrey, T., Jr., Bohrer, J. J. and Mark, H., *Copolymerization*, Interscience Publishers, New York City (1952)

## Fibers

28. Hermans, P. H., *Physics and Chemistry of Cellulose Fibres*, Elsevier Pub. Co., New York City (1949)

29. Hill, R., Ed., *Fibres from Synthetic Polymers*, Elsevier Pub. Co., New York City (1953)

30. Kratky, O., *Chemische Textilfasern*, Encke, Stuttgart (1951)

31. McFarlane, S. B., *Technology of Synthetic Fibers*, Fairchild Publications, Inc., New York City (1953)

## Physical Properties

32. Alfrey, T., Jr., *Mechanical Behavior of High Polymers*, Interscience Publishers, New York City (1948)

33. Houwink, R., *Elasticity, Plasticity, and Structure of Matter*, Cambridge University Press, Cambridge, England (1937)

34. van de Hulst, H. C., *Light Scattering by Small Particles*, John Wiley and Sons, Inc., New York City (1957)

## Physics

35. Hermans, P. H., *Contributions to the Physics of Cellulose Fibres*, Elsevier Pub. Co., New York City (1946)

36. Robinson, H. A., Ed., *High-Polymer Physics*, Chemical Pub. Co., New York City (1948)

37. Stuart, H. A., *The Physics of High Polymers*, Springer-Verlag, Berlin (1956)

38. Treloar, L. R. G., *The Physics of Rubber Elasticity*, Clarendon Press, Oxford (1949)

## Plastics

39. Barron, H., *Modern Synthetic Plastics,* D. Van Nostrand Co., New York City (1945)

40. Boundy, R. H. and Boyer, R. F., *Styrene—Its Polymers, Copolymers and Derivatives,* Reinhold Pub. Corp., New York City (1952)

41. Buttrey, D. N., *Cellulose Plastics,* Cleaver-Hume Press, Ltd., London (1947)

42. D'Alelio, G. F., *Experimental Plastics and Synthetic Resins* (2nd Ed.), John Wiley and Sons, Inc., New York City (1946)

43. Fleck, H. R., *Plastics—Scientific and Technological* (3rd and 1st Eds. respectively), Chemical Pub. Co., New York City (1951 and 1945)

44. Jellinek, H. H. G., *Degradation of Vinyl Polymers,* Academic Press, New York City (1955)

45. MacTaggart, E. F. and Chambers, H. H., *Plastics and Building,* Philosophical Lib., New York City (1955)

46. Mark, H. and Proskauer, E. S., Eds., *The Science of Plastics,* Interscience Publishers, New York City (1948)

47. Ritchie, P. D., *A Chemistry of Plastics and High Polymers,* Cleaver-Hume Press, Ltd., London (1949)

48. Schildknecht, C. E., *Vinyl and Related Polymers,* John Wiley and Sons, Inc., New York City (1952)

49. Winding, C. C. and Hasche, R. L., *Plastics: Theory and Practice—Chemical Engineering Series,* McGraw-Hill Book Co., New York City (1947)

## Polyamides

50. Mark, H. and Whitby, G. S., Eds., *Collected Papers of Wallace Hume Carothers,* Interscience Publishers, New York City (1940)

50a. Floyd, D. E., *Polyamide Resins,* Reinhold Publishing Corporation, New York City (1957)

## Polyethylene

51. Bjorksten, J., Ed., *Polyesters and Their Applications,* Reinhold Pub. Corp., New York City (1956)

52. Kresser, T. O. J., *Polyethylene,* Reinhold Pub. Corp., New York City (1957)

53. Raff, R. A. V. and Allison, J. B., *Polyethylene,* Interscience Publishers, New York City (1956)

## Polymerization

54. Bovey, F. A., Kolthoff, I. M., Medalia, A. I. and Meehan, E. G., *Emulsion Polymerization,* Interscience Publishers, New York City (1955)

55. D'Alelio, G. F., *Fundamental Principles of Polymerization, Rubbers, Plastics, and Fibers*, John Wiley and Sons, Inc., New York City (1952)
56. Plesch, P. H., *Cationic Polymerization and Related Complexes*, Academic Press, New York City (1954)
57. Schildknecht, C. E., ed., *High Polymers*, (Vol. X: *Polymer Processes*), Interscience Publishers, New York City (1956)

### Proteins

58. Anson, M. L. and Edsall, J. T., Eds., *Advances in Protein Chemistry* (Vol. I), Academic Press, New York City (1944)
59. Bamford, C. H., Elliott, A., and Hanby, W. A., *Synthetic Polypeptides* (Vol. 5 of Physical Chemistry Series), Academic Press, New York City (1956)
60. Cohn, E. J. and Edsall, J. T., *Proteins, Amino Acids and Peptides*, Reinhold Pub. Corp., New York City (1943)
61. Neurath, H. and Bailey, K., Eds., *The Proteins: Chemistry, Biological Activity and Methods* (Vols. 1A, 1B, 2A and 2B), Academic Press, New York City (1953)

### Resins

62. Carswell, T. S., *Phenoplasts: Their Structure, Properties, and Chemical Technology*, Interscience Publishers, New York City (1947)
63. Mantell, C. L., Kopf, C. W., Curtis, J. L. and Rogers, E. M., *The Technology of Natural Resins* (1st Ed.), John Wiley and Sons, Inc., New York City (1942)
64. Martin, R. W., *The Chemistry of Phenolic Resins*, John Wiley and Sons, Inc., New York City (1956)
65. Morrell, R. S. (3rd Ed. by H. M. Langton), *Synthetic Resins and Allied Plastics*, Oxford Univ. Press, London (1951)
66. Powers, P. O., *Synthetic Resins and Plastics* (1st Ed.), John Wiley and Sons, Inc., New York City (1943)

### Rubbers

67. Bunn, C. W., Mark, H. and Whitby, G. S., Eds., *The Study of Rubber-like Substances by X-ray Diffraction Methods, in Scientif. Progress in the Field of Rubber and Synthetic Elastomers* (Advances in Colloid Science, Vol. II), Interscience Publishers, New York City (1946)
68. Cook, P. G., *Latex—Natural and Synthetic*, Reinhold Pub. Corp., New York City (1956)
69. Davis, C. C. and Blake, J. T., Eds., *The Chemistry and Technology of Rubber*, Reinhold Pub. Corp., New York City (1937)

70. Fisher, Harry, *Chemistry of Natural and Synthetic Rubbers*, Reinhold Pub. Corp., New York City (1957)
71. Flint, C. F., *The Chemistry and Technology of Rubber Latex*, D. Van Nostrand Co., New York City (1938)
72. Gee, G., *Thermodynamics of Rubber Solutions and Gels, in Advances in Colloid Science* (Vol. II), Interscience Publishers, New York City (1946)
73. Whitby, G. S., Davis, C. C. and Dunbrook, R. F., Eds., *Synthetic Rubber*, John Wiley and Sons, Inc., New York City (1954)
74. Wildschut, A. J., *Technological and Physical Investigations on Natural and Synthetic Rubbers* (1st Ed.), Elsevier Pub. Co., New York City (1946)

## Silicones

75. McGregor, R. R., *Silicones and Their Uses*, McGraw-Hill Book Co., New York City (1954)
76. Rochow, E. G., *An Introduction to the Chemistry of the Silicones* (2nd Ed.), John Wiley and Sons, Inc., New York City (1951)
77. Post, H. W., *Silicones and Other Organic Silicon Compounds*, Reinhold Pub. Corp., New York City (1949)

## General High Polymer Textbooks

78. Burnett, G. M., *Mechanisms of Polymer Reactions*, Interscience Publishers, New York City (1954)
79. Frith, E. M. and Tuckett, R. F., *Linear Polymers*, Longmans, Green and Co., New York City (1951)
80. Grassie, N., *Chemistry of High Polymer Degradation Processes*, Interscience Publishers, New York City (1956)
81. Houwink, R., *Technology of Synthetic Polymers*, Elsevier Pub. Co., New York City (1947)
82. Houwink, R., *Fundamentals of Synthetic Polymer Technology*, Elsevier Pub. Co., New York City (1949)
83. Mark, H. and Raff, R., *High Polymer Reactions*, Interscience Publishers, New York City (1941)
84. Meyer, K. H., *Natural and Synthetic High Polymers* (High Polymers, Vol. IV), 2nd Ed., Interscience Publishers, New York City (1950)
85. Roff, W. J., *Fibres, Plastics, and Rubbers*, Academic Press, New York City (1956)
86. Schildknecht, C. E., *Polymer Processes*, Interscience Publishers, New York City (1956)
87. Schmidt, A. X. and Marlies, C. A., *Principles of High Polymer Theory and Practice*, McGraw-Hill Book Co., New York City (1948)

88. Staudinger, H., *Die Hochmolekularen Organischen Verbindungen,* Julius Springer, Berlin (1932)

89. Twiss, S. B., *Advancing Fronts in Chemistry* (Vol. I, High Polymers), Reinhold Pub. Corp., New York City (1945)

# Index